The Edges of Twilight

An artistic interpretation of the music
of The Tea Party

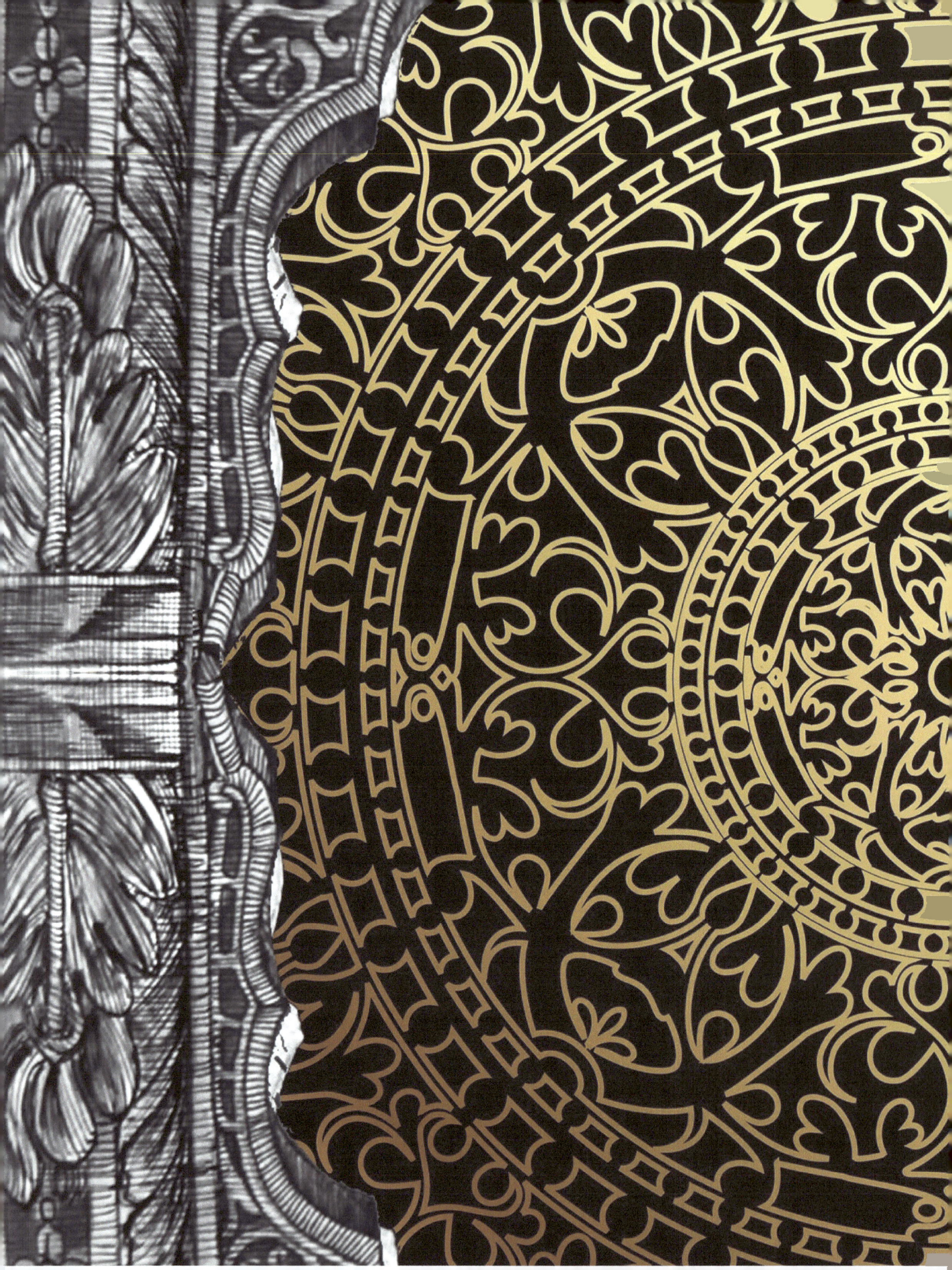

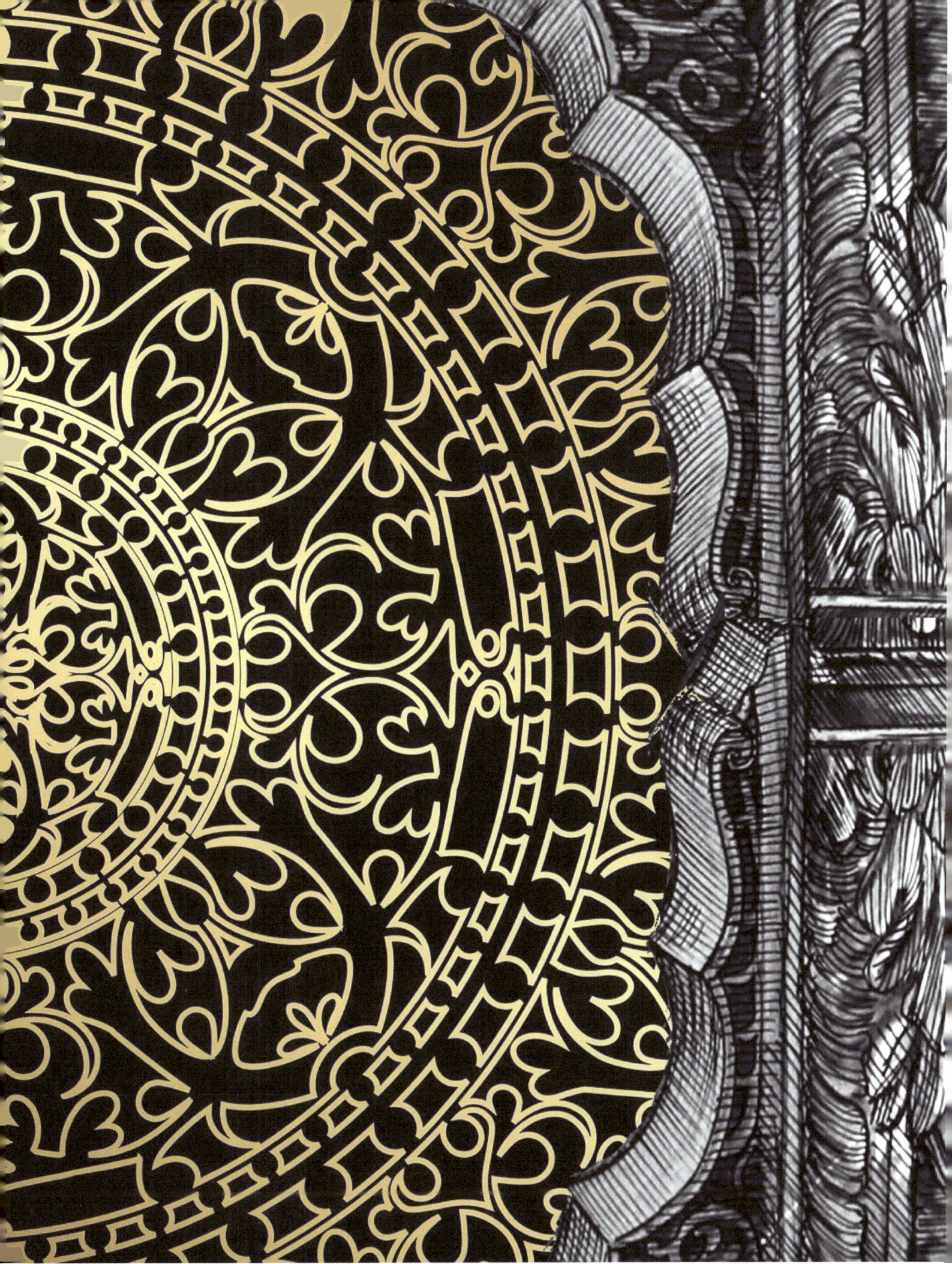

The Edges of Twilight: Artistic interpretations of the music of The Tea Party
This publication was created to celebrate the 20th anniversary of 'The Edges of Twilight' album written by
Jeff Martin, Stuart Chatwood and Jeff Burrows.

Published by Buratti Creative
ISBN 978-0992499198

www.robertburatti.com
www.teaparty.com

The Edges of Twilight

An artistic interpretation of the music
of The Tea Party

Lyrics by Jeff Martin
Artwork by Robert Buratti

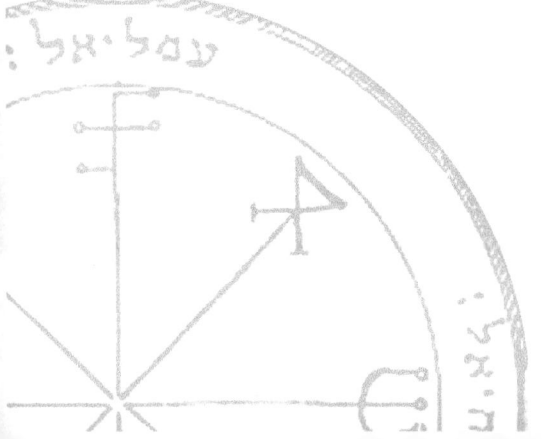

6

Contents

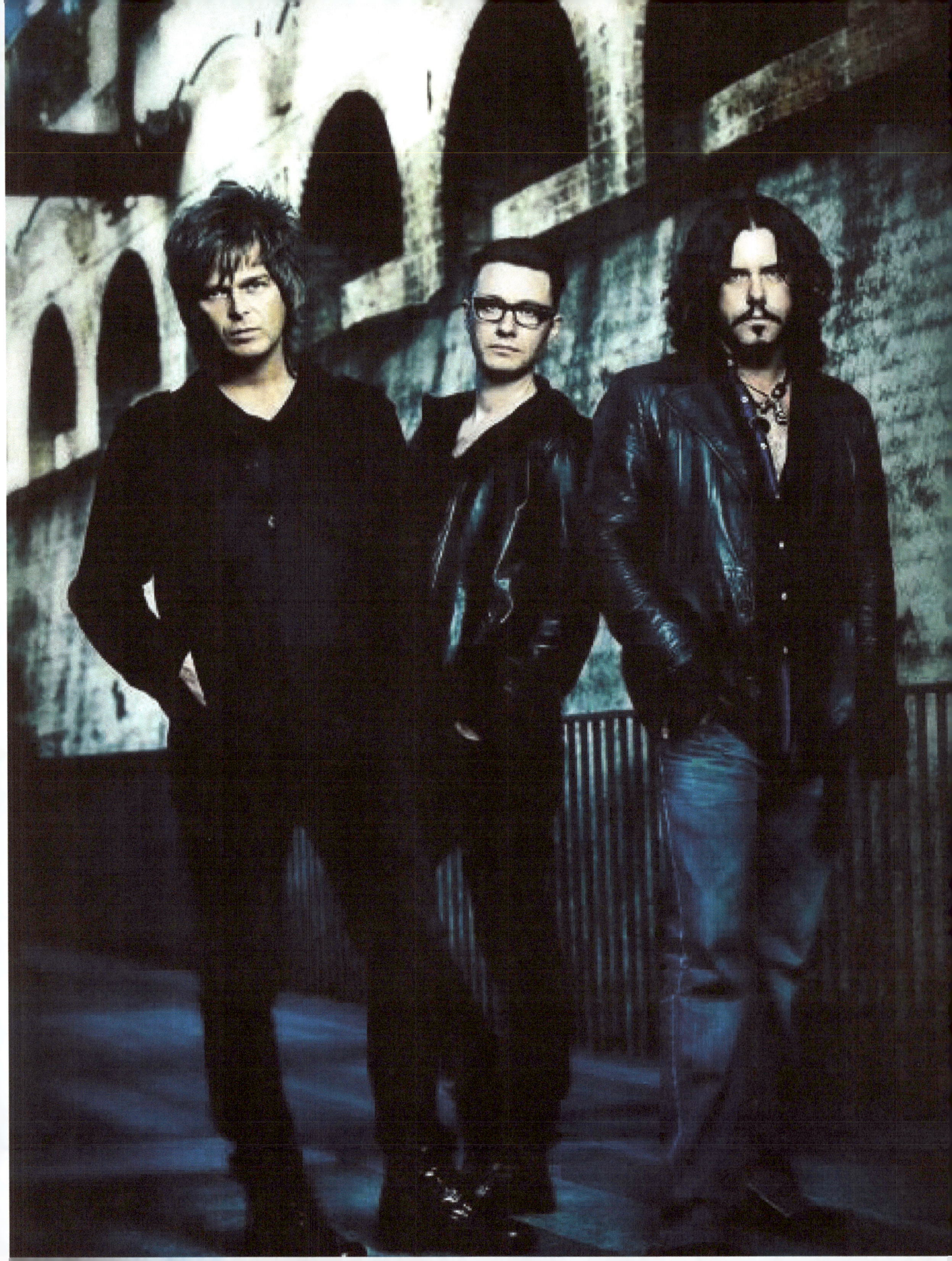

Introduction

The Tea Party was formed in 1990 by Jeff Martin, Stuart Chatwood and Jeff Burrows after a marathon jam session at the Cherry Beach Rehearsal Studios in Toronto. Each member had previously played together during their teenage years in a number of different bands in Windsor, Ontario, where they were originally from. They had decided to name their new group *The Tea Party* after the infamous hash sessions of famous Beat generation poets Allen Ginsberg, Jack Kerouac and William Burroughs.

The Tea Party released their eponymous debut album in 1991, distributing it through their own label Eternal Discs. The album drew influences from psychedelic rock and blues, and was produced by Martin; album production was something Martin would continue with for all of The Tea Party's albums, as a way of giving the band complete artistic control. In 1993 The Tea Party signed to EMI Music Canada and released their first major label recording, *Splendor Solis*. The band employed open tunings and goblet drums (Dumbek) to create Indian-style sounds, something they continued to employ throughout their career, while continuing in a blues influenced style. In 1994 the album released in Australia, with the single *Save Me* launching the band's career in the country. The band gained the support of national radio station Triple J, enabling the band's first tour, with *Save Me* becoming a staple of their setlists.

Further developing The Tea Party's sound in 1995, *The Edges of Twilight* was recorded with an array of Indian and Middle-eastern instrumentation. Jeff Burrows explained that *"basically we wanted to expand upon the initial idea that we tried on Splendor Solis, which was trying to incorporate different styles of world music into our music. So with this album we became more familiar with many more instruments. In our minds we were trying to do for a rock album what Peter Gabriel does to pop by infusing various cultures, percussion and exotic sounds into it."*

The title of the album is taken from a chapter of the book *Fire in the Head*, by the American author Tom Cowan, which also inspired the name of the first track. The album also included a hidden song which features a spoken word performance by the folk legend Roy Harper, who is a friend of the band. On the cover is a statue by William Wetmore Story called *Angel of Grief*.

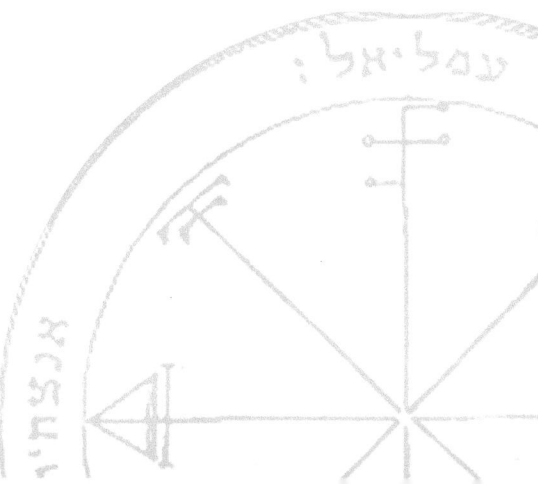

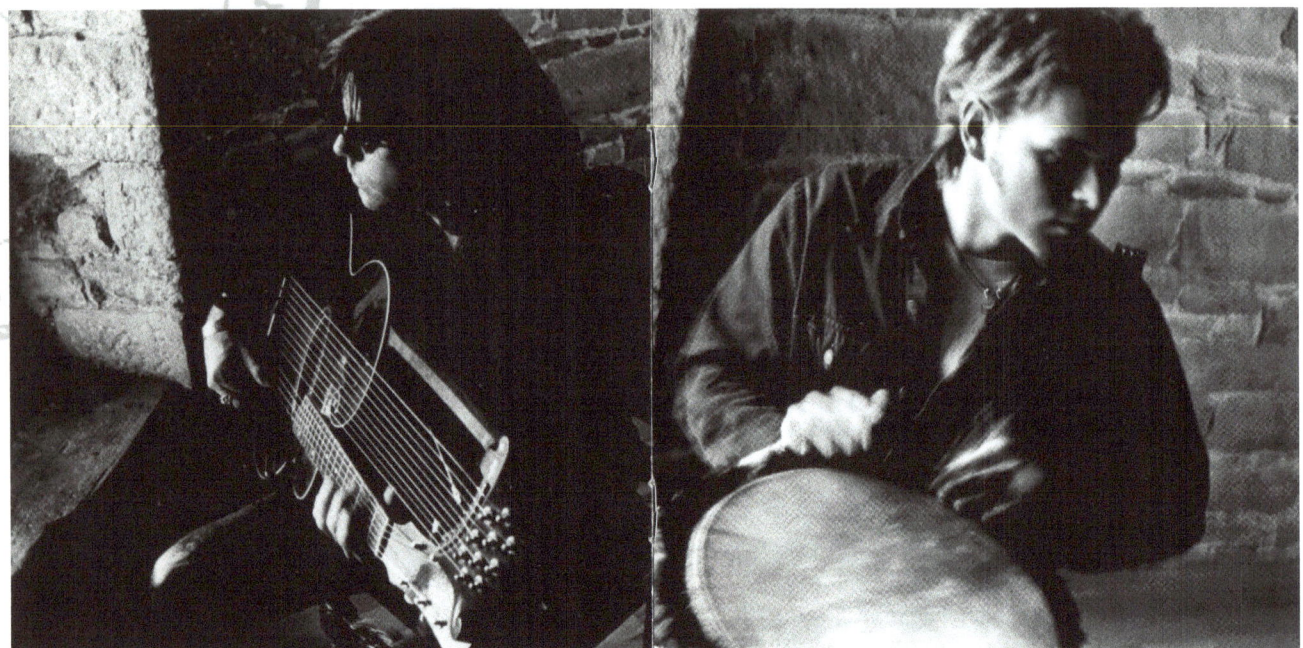

Sister Awake, the third single from the album, defines what the band set out to do, combining three-piece rock compositions with music from the world. *Sister Awake* is an acoustically based arrangement on 12-string guitar, sitar, sarod, harmonium and goblet drums. *The Edges of Twilight* is The Tea Party's most commercially successful album; with sales exceeding 270,000 units, the album is certified double platinum in Canada and platinum in Australia. The album helped propel the band into mainstream success in their native Canada, where it reached double platinum status and earned the band several Juno nominations, including "Best Rock Album" and "Group of the Year".

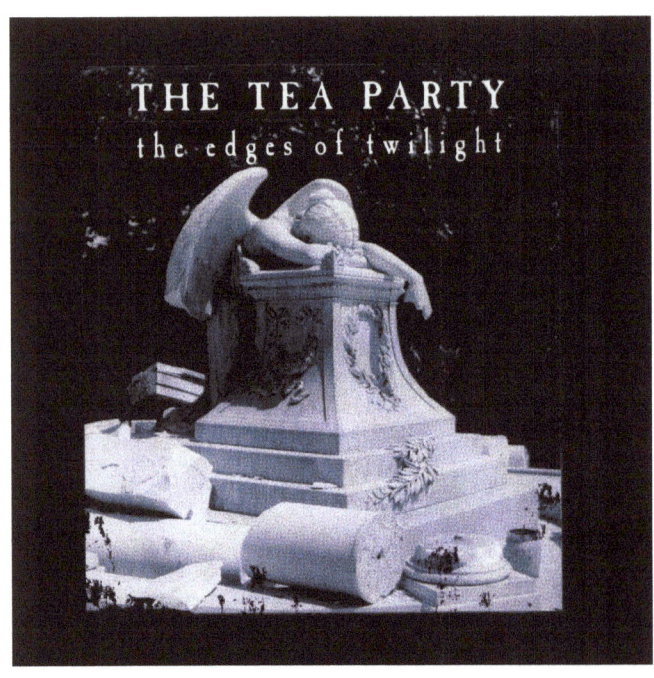

To commemorate the 20th anniversary of The Edges of Twilight, The Tea Party released a deluxe remastered CD, remastered LP, and a North American tour. The deluxe CD also includes a bonus disc that includes alternate, live, radio sessions and bonus audio and the booklet features the story of the album with new band interviews and previously unseen photos. A series of original artworks were commissioned by the band from Australian artist, Robert Buratti which were released worldwide.

Buratti also created a series of short films which were projected as a backdrop to the band while performing across Canada and Australia.

(right) Robert Buratti, *The Edges of Twilight* pen and ink on paper   40 x 30cm (top) Images from original CD insert

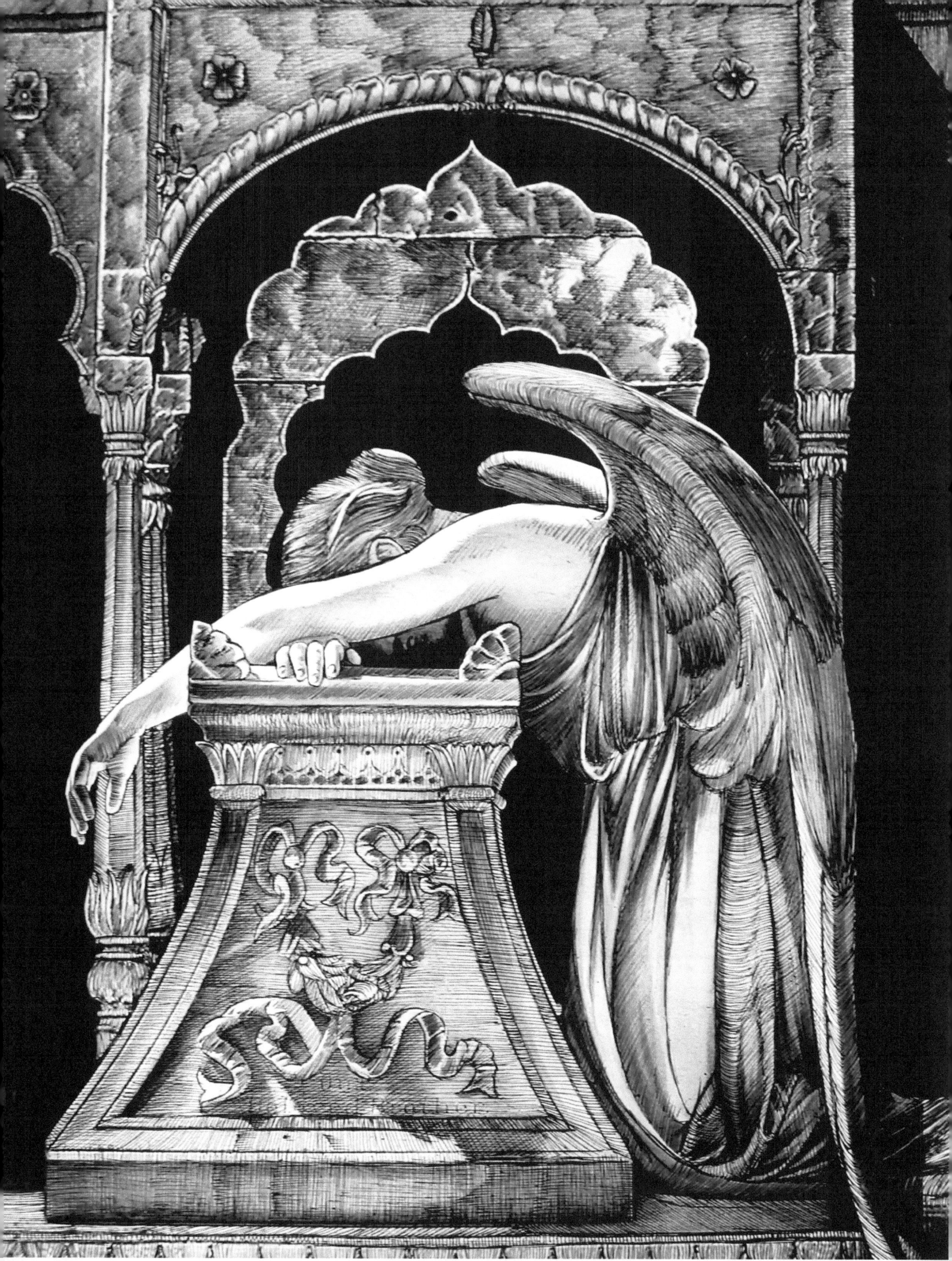

Fire in the Head

You stay
Silent, knowing, always in time
See how this love stays divine
Sleep here
Hoping, knowing, always in time
See how this loves stays divine

This is the way step inside
and I'm waiting
When I return to her I find
I'm waiting
Flowers of evil in my mind
and I'm waiting
Dancing with fire on the edge

I'm waiting
Remembering all of what she said
and i'm waiting
Hoping the rains will wash away
I'm waiting
Hoping a guide will show the way
and I'm waiting
Dancing with fire on the edge
I'm waiting
Remembering all of what she said
with this fire in my head

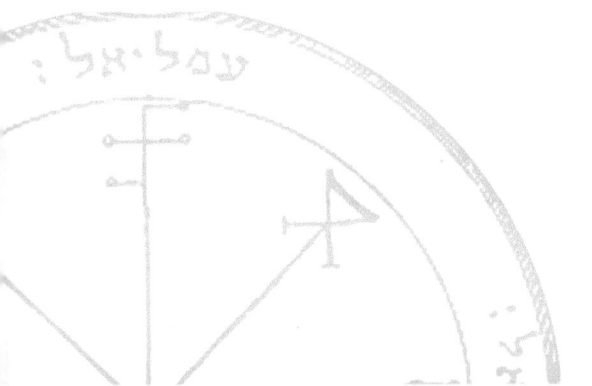

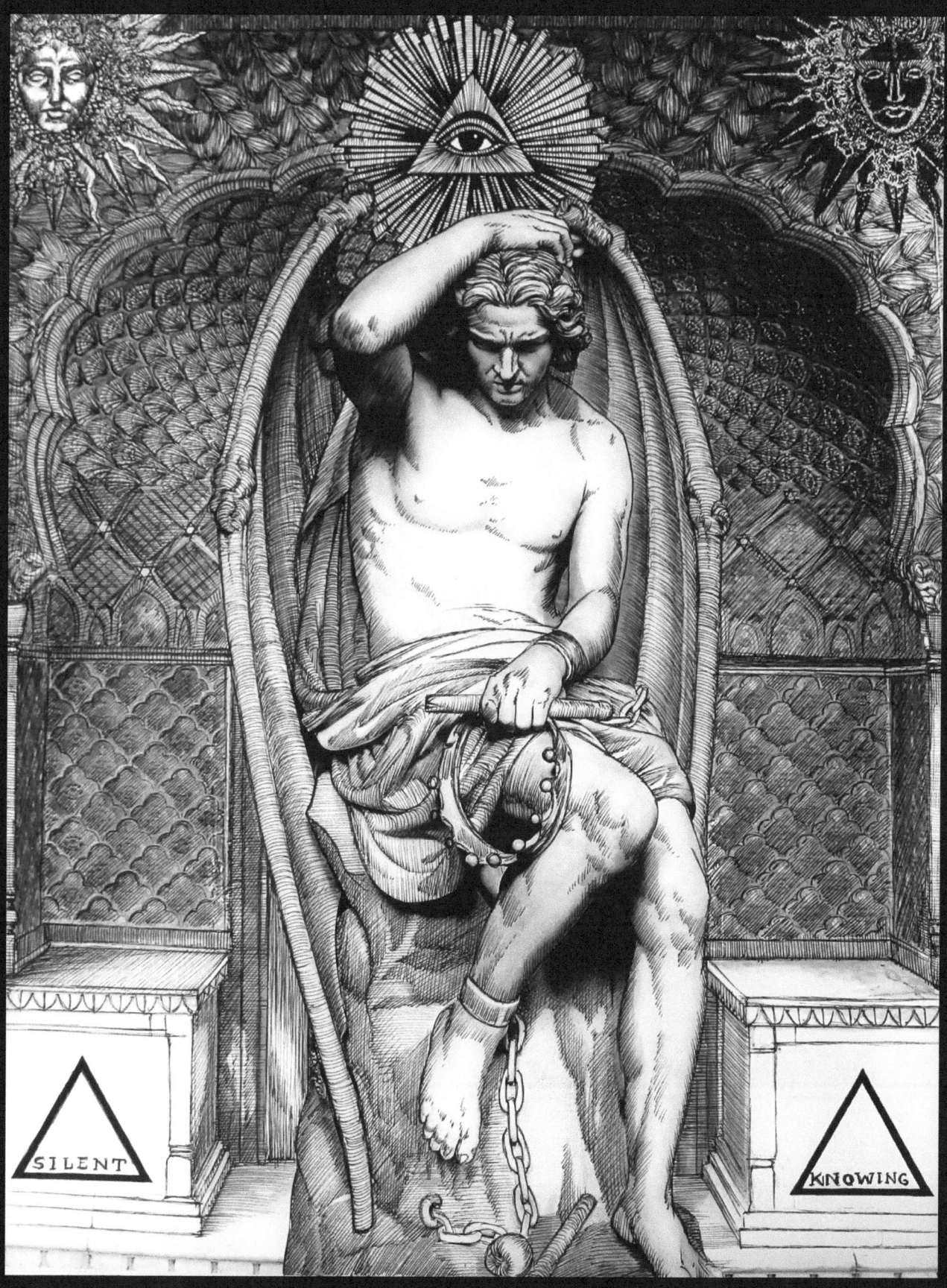

Fire in the Head   pen and ink on paper   40 x 30cm

The Bazaar

Silence swimming in a pool of dreams
Beneath its depths the forgotten streams
Above, the city of the evening star
behind its wall, the grand bazaar
As she walks through it endless maze
Cursing those who mistrust her ways
Please my friend no matter what she sees
Tell my lover come back to me

Doorways spilling out their sombre light
Casting shadows that will raid the night
Along the alleys of her ruling fears
Walk the visions that will cause her tears
Lying still as she wills her glance

Through the eyes of a charmer's trance
Please my friend no matter what she sees
Tell my lover come back to me

And on the walls
Shadows play
Twilight souls
Anguished ways
Lost adrift
Severed seas
I await you

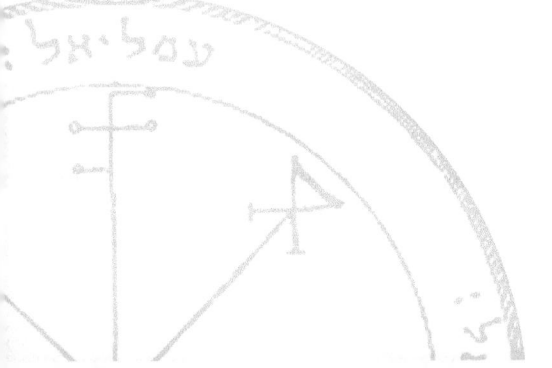

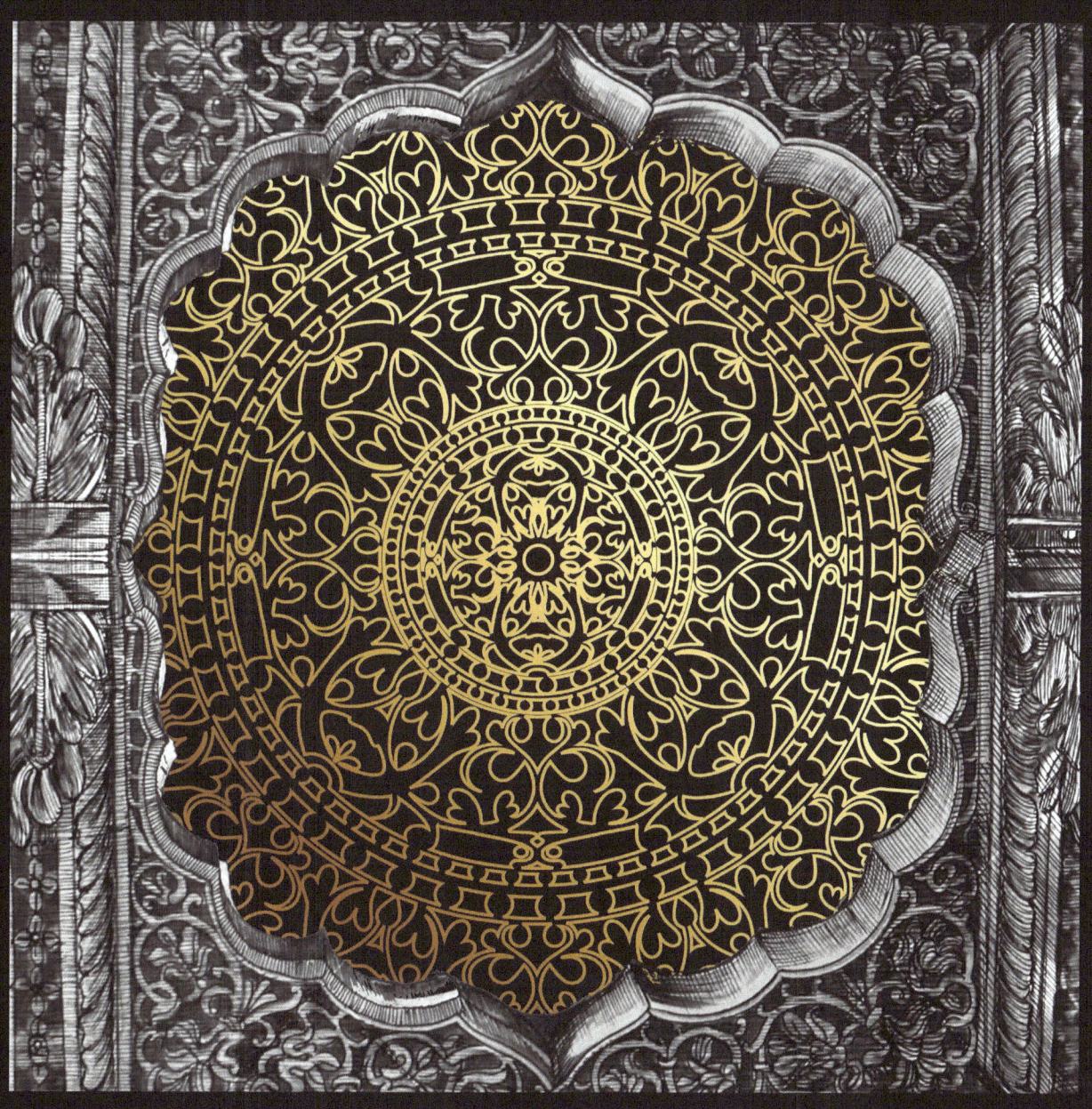

The Bazaar   pen and ink on paper   40 x 40cm

Correspondences

Hope springs to life
Charmed by approaching listlessness
Hands reaching out
To grasp the open emptiness

Leading me down...

And this goodbye
Faced with hope and countenance
Souls slip away
To bask in glowing radiance

Leading me down...

As we run from the sun
And we harbour the lies
And we leave things undone

As we cover our eyes

Does it tear you apart my love
Does it tear you apart my love
It tears me apart

Charmed by this light
This sombre guidance in her eyes
Rage would entice
And final moments would arise

Leading me down...

Does it tear you apart my love
Does it tear you apart my love
It tears me apart

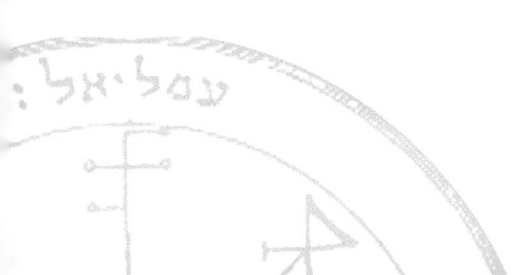

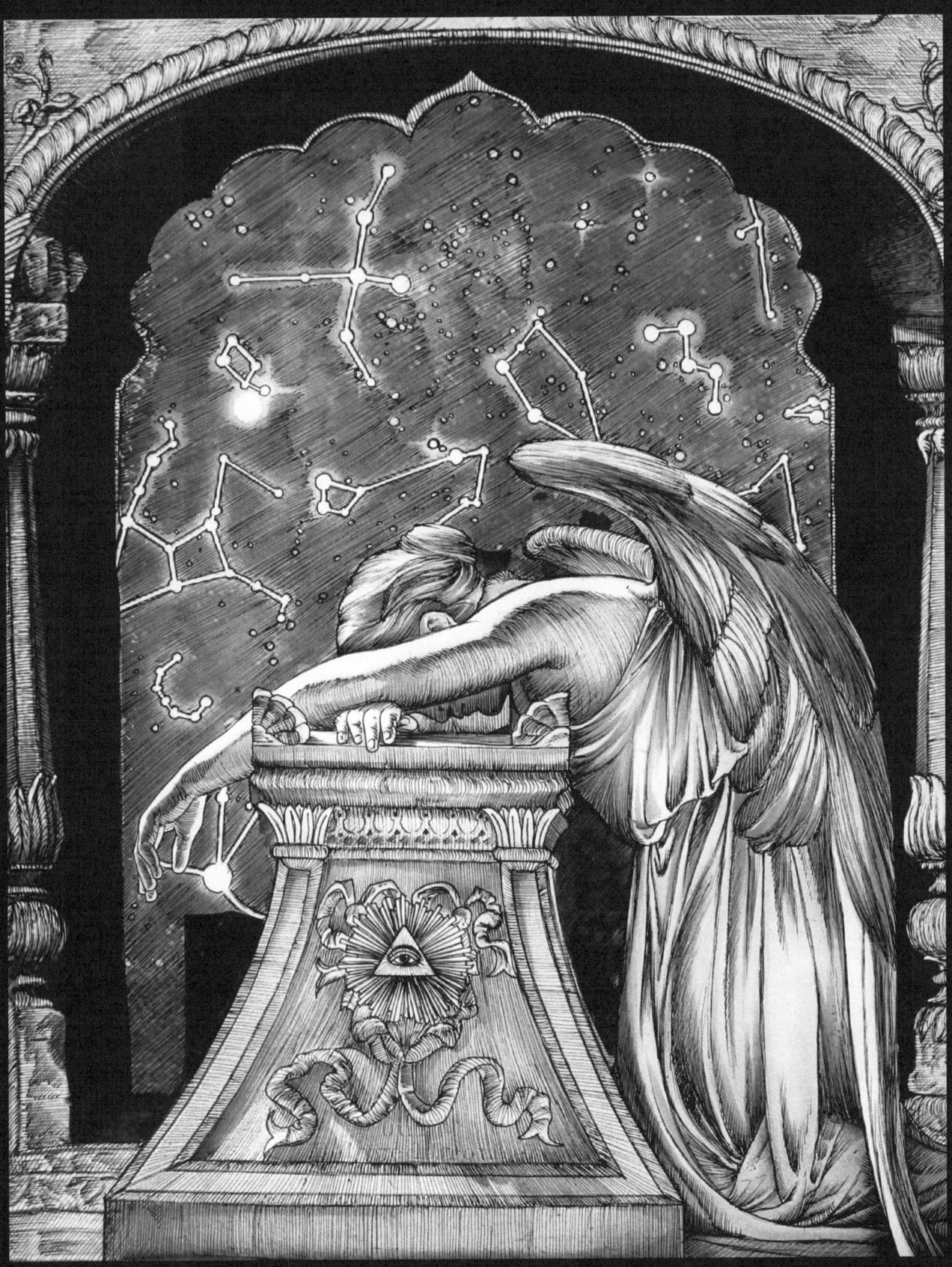

Correspondences pen and ink on paper 40 x 30cm

The Badger

Instrumental

According to Native Americans, the sighting of badger tracks was very auspicious. Seeing badger tracks was a message that all things are possible when we tap into our inner creative powers.

The badger stops at nothing to get what it wants, and this is a lesson for us to be persistent in our pursuits.

The badger is fiercely independent and aggressive when threatened. He teaches the lesson of standing our ground and making our presence known when the situation calls for it.

The Badger is connected to the earth which means that it is a grounding totem. When we feel out of touch, the Badger can help us get rooted within ourselves, and anchor us to what is important in our lives.

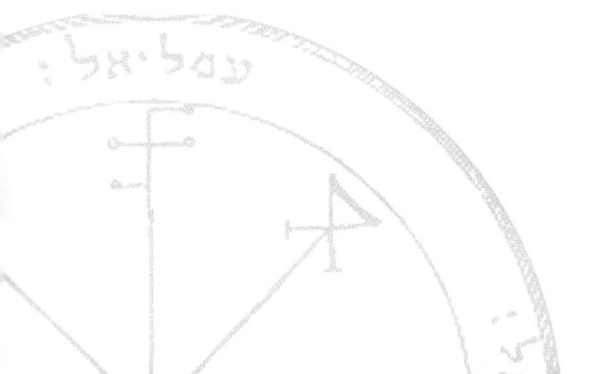

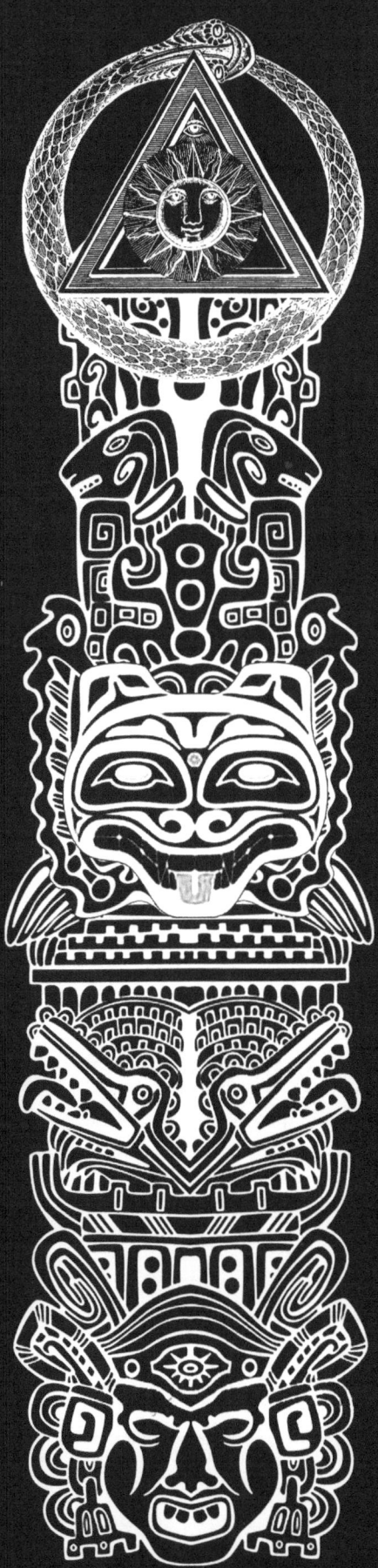

The Badger   pen and ink on paper   40 x 10cm

Silence

Silent spirit
walks before me
with her beauty
and with her eyes
Heaven help me
I feel I'm fading
I should rest here for a while

In the dreamtime
I'm awakened
as my senses
seize the night

Heaven help me
I'm forsaken
I should rest here for a while

And lie in the bed you've made ophelia
Dry are the lips that lost their taste of love
Drown in the waters that would give you life
Cry as this lamentation thrusts its knife

In silence
In silence

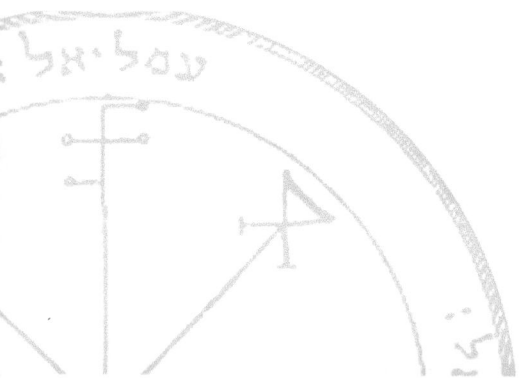

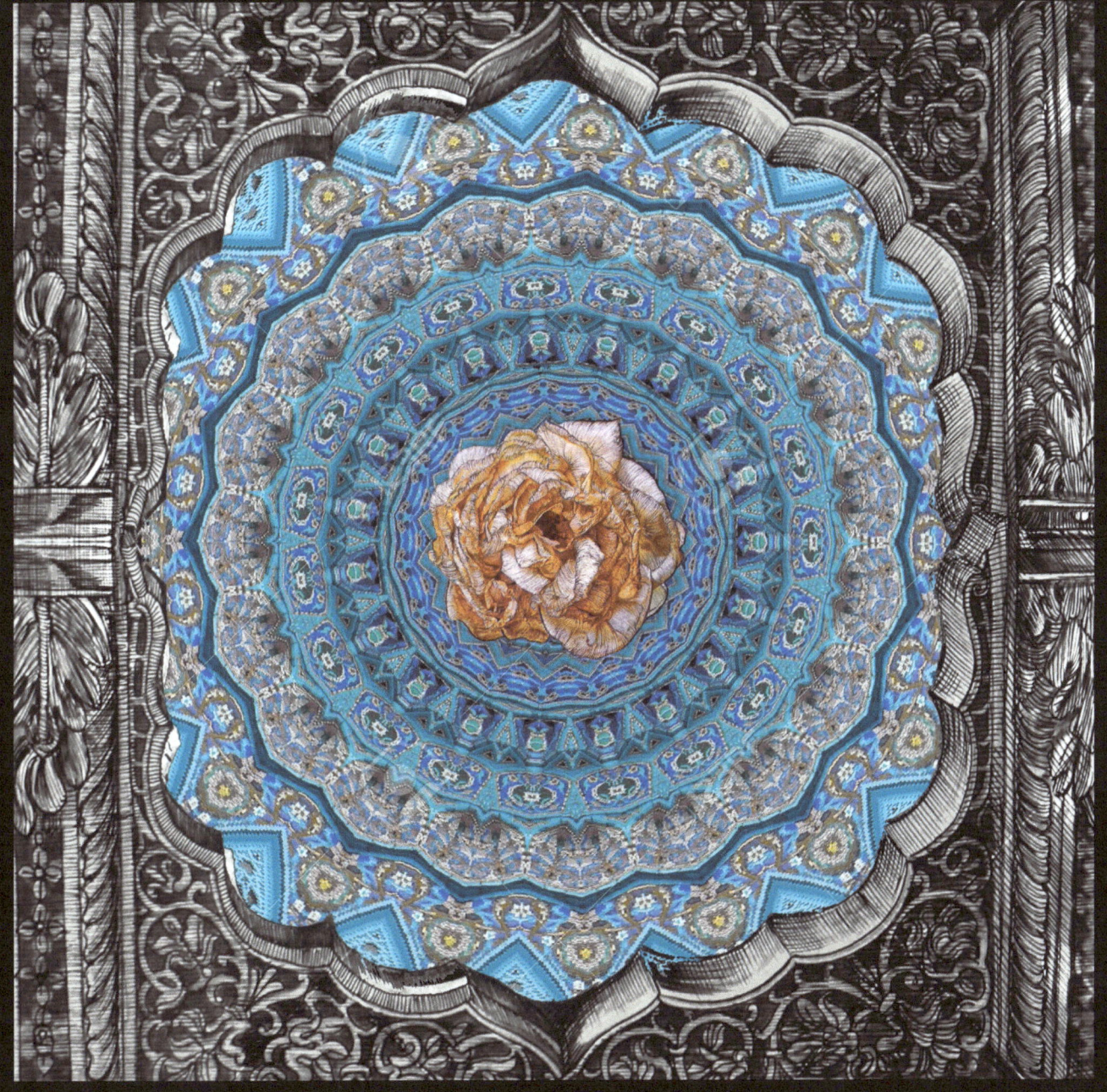

Silence   pen and ink on paper   40 x 40cm

Sister Awake

When the winter was over
she returned there to find him
and her memories filled her with light

She remembered the beauty
She remembered desires
and her memories filled her with light

I am the sun in the flame
cold from the flame turns away
and in these winds came a change
she awakes...

Sister walk through these fields of delight
but I want you to know
Desperation's the tenderest trap
so gently you go
What will it take sister awake

When this beautiful cult of desire
has left you for dead
Isolation will cradle the lies
of things left unsaid
What will it take sister awake

And you'll look to the heavens above
and taste its deceit
These temptations have blinded desires
to sleep at their feet
What will it take sister awake

And you'll hear them call out your name
invoking the fates
Chances are you've travelled too far
in stirring their hate

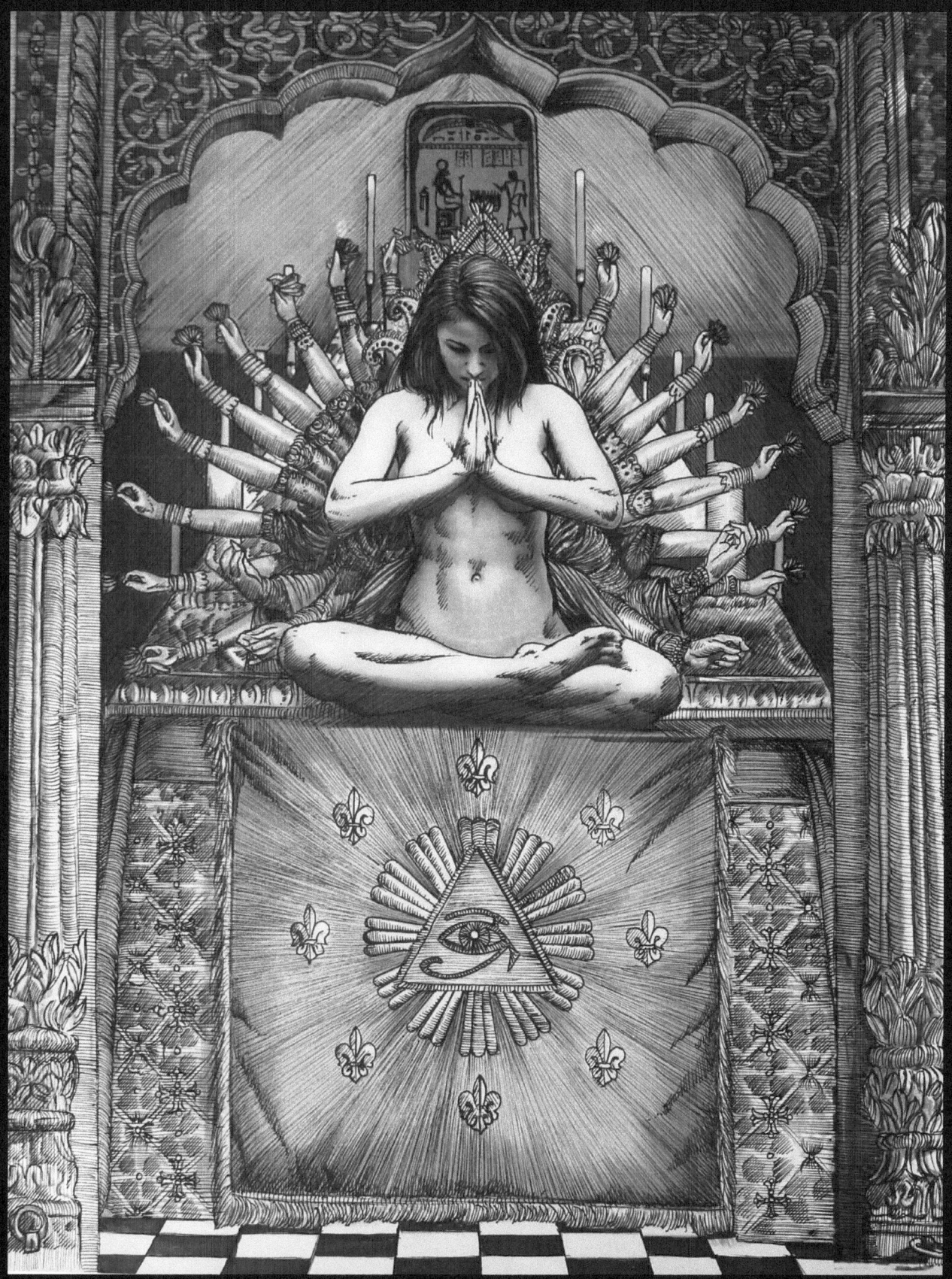

Sister Awake   pen and ink on paper   40 x 30cm

Turn The Lamp Down Low

Turn the lamp down low
Baby shelter me
Turn the lamp down low
Bright enough to see
Turn the lamp down low
Please don't go

Do you feel a flame that's burning
as the candle dies
Do you see the spirits stirring
as you close your eyes
Do you sense the slow advancement
as the twilight thins
Do you see the serpent dancing
as it sheds its skin

Turn the lamp down low
Baby please don't go

Does the sun renounce its kingdom

As the shadows fall
Does a fool rejoice in wisdom
when the raven calls
Do you embrace the dancing clayman
as he tears your flesh
Do you hear the souls screaming
in the serpents mesh

Turn the lamp down low
Baby please don't go

Do you need the consolation
of a dead man's hand
Aas the tears of desolation
flood a dead man's land
Do you seek your souls redemption
under fervent skies
Don't you see your own reflection
in the serpent's eye

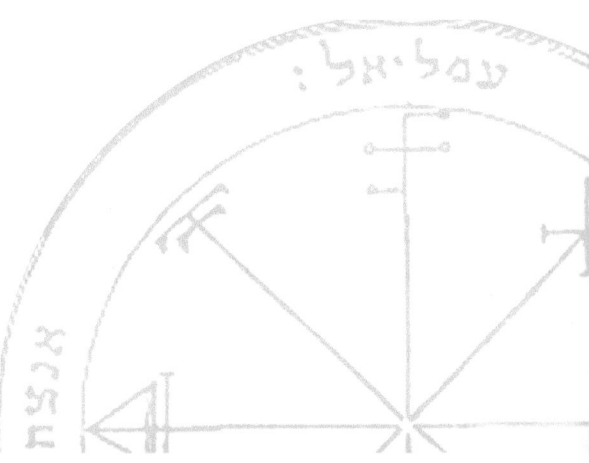

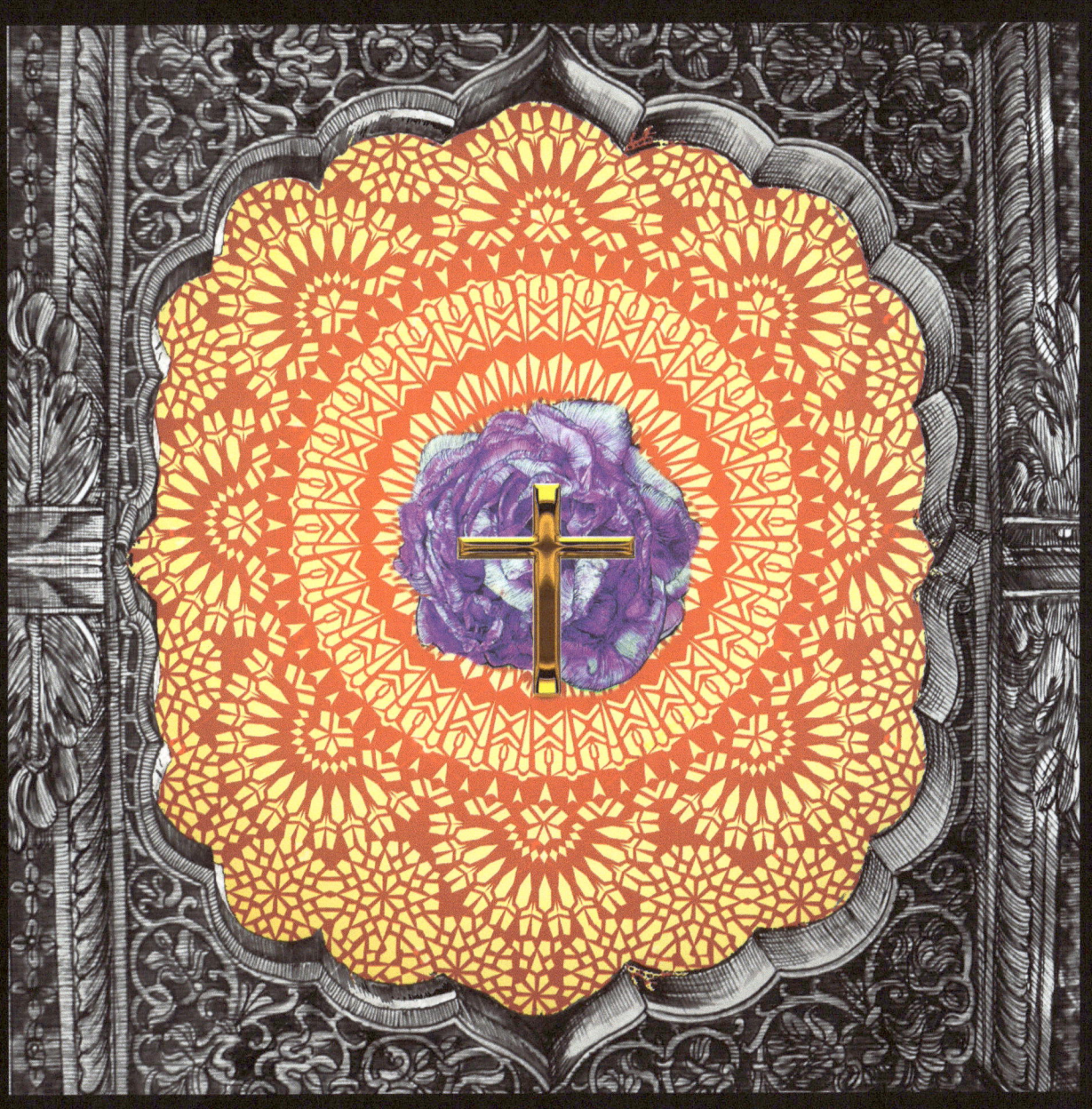

Turn the Lamp Down Low   pen and ink on paper   40 x 40cm

Shadows On The Mountainside

We are spirits passing through the doors of time
with an invitation heard before we find
Shadows on the mountainside
eagles find the souls they hide

And the outcast child enchanted by the sun
will he seek his shelter never knowing one
Shadows on the mountainside
eagles find the souls they hide

Shadows on the mountainside
cover me with sleep

because I need it now

And the red rivers flow
to seas
And she will return
to me
And then all that I am
is in her hands
And I will return to her
And then I begin

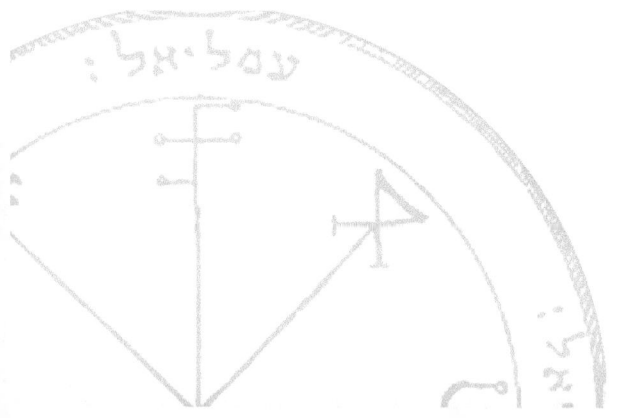

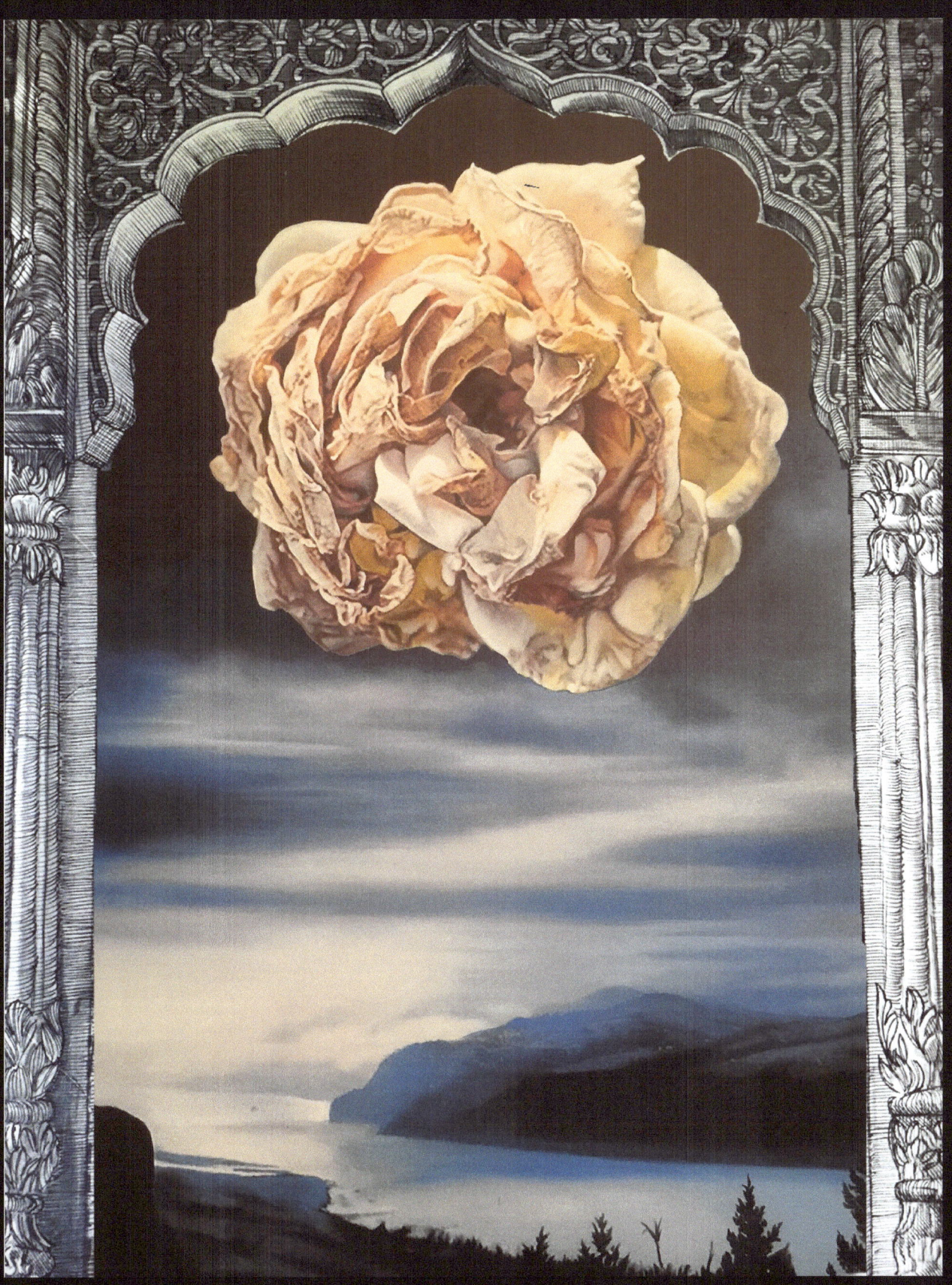

Shadows on the Mountainside   oil, pen and ink on paper   40 x 30cm

Drawing Down The Moon

Holding on once again
take the time to look around
Is it all in vain
Can't you see stay with me

I need you now
to stop the rains baby
But you can't see how it feels
until you have felt the same
Can't you see
Stay with me

Don't let me down
stay with me
Don't leave me now
stay with me
When darkness descends
it's all you see
Don't let me down
stay with me

She's drawing down the moon
I can see it in her eyes
I think it's too soon
I think I heard her cry
She's drawing down the moon
I can see her walk away
I think its too soon
Can't she hear me when I say

You gota tell me what you wan't
Don't let me down
Stay with me
Don't leave me now
Stay with me
When darkness descends
It's all we'll see

28

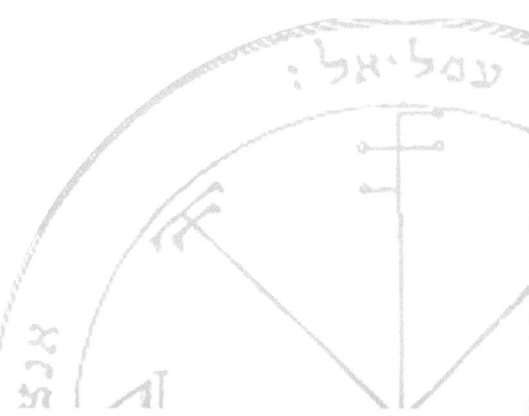

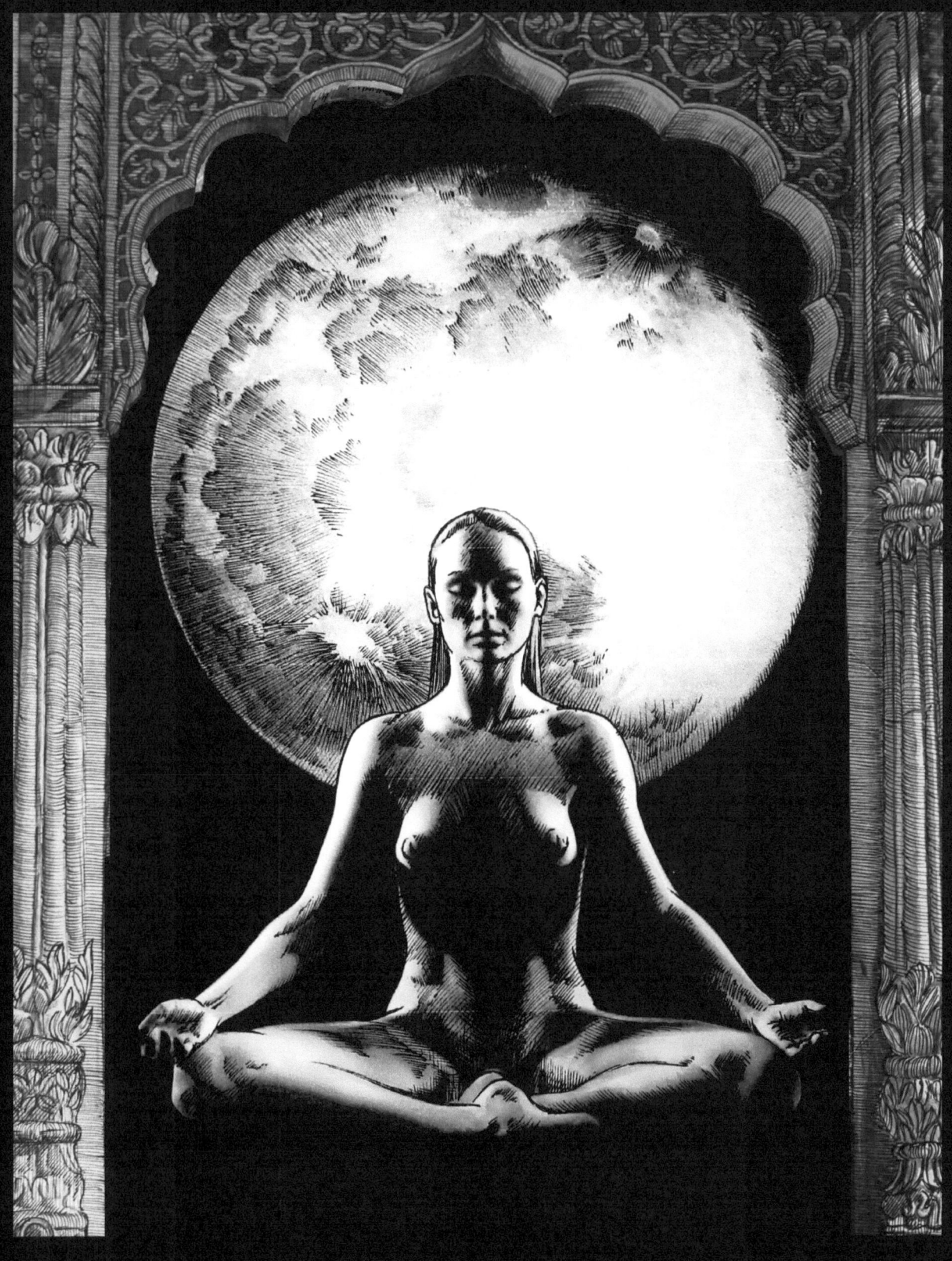

Drawing Down the Moon pen and ink on paper   40 x 30cm

Inanna

Over the skies and sea my love
Over the sky and sea
Riding the crest of winds
above bringing her back to me

Into the starlit sea my love
Into the moonlit sea

Riding the crest of winds above
I'm begging you stay with me

Would you walk ten miles with me my love
Would you walk the skies with me
Would you walk ten miles with me my love
Inanna

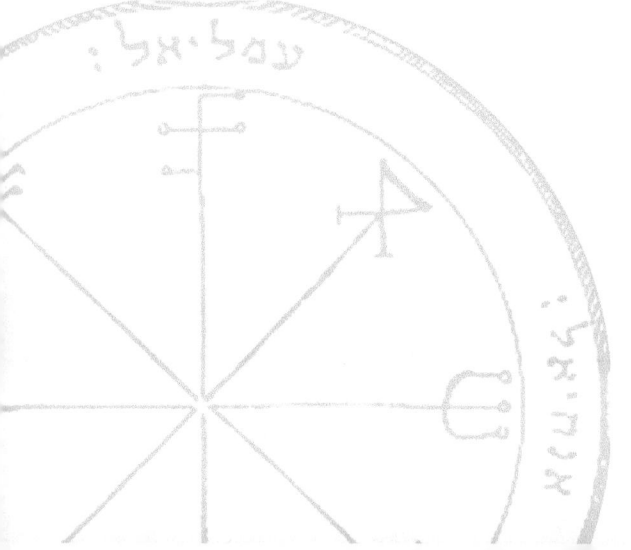

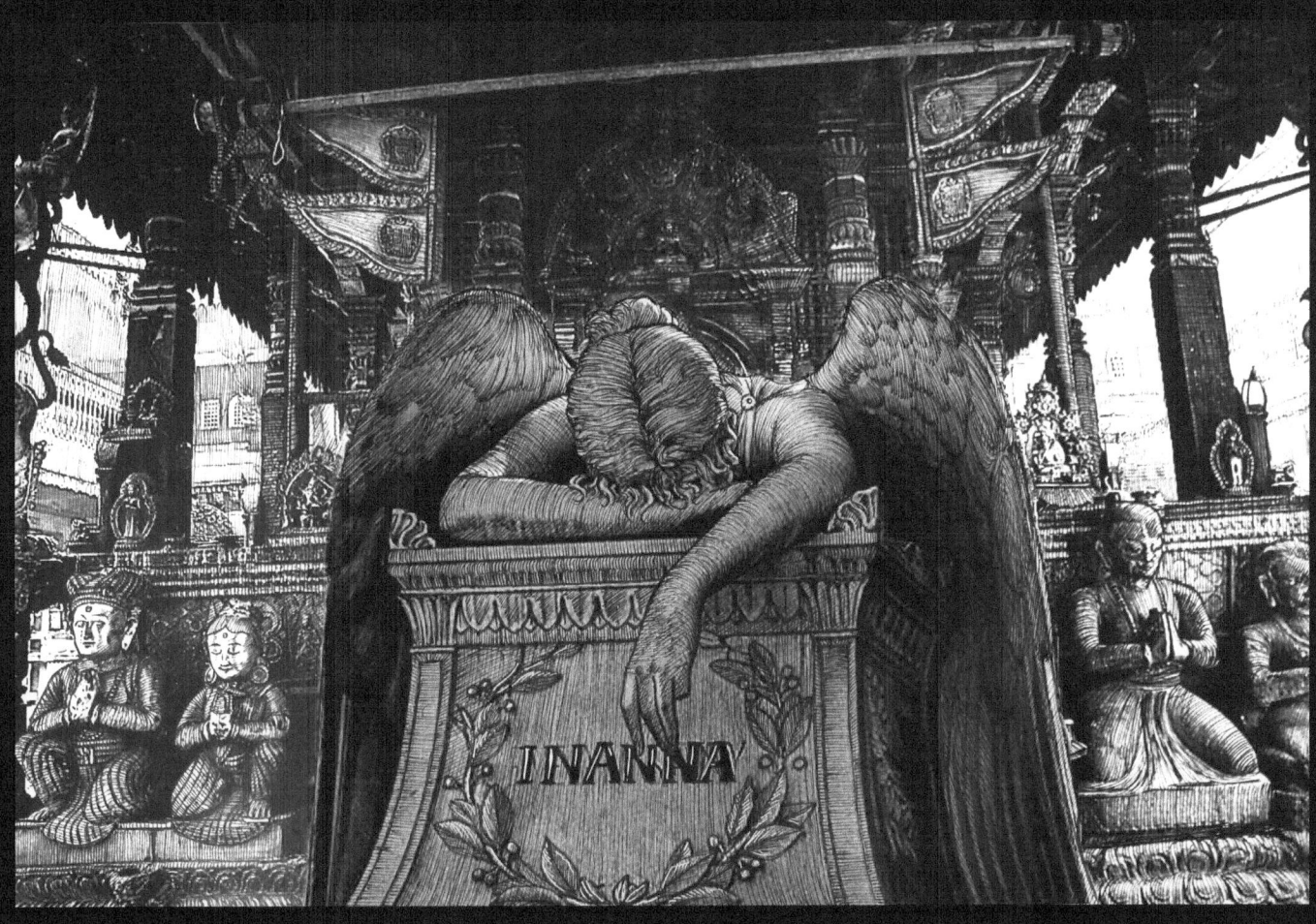

Inanna pen and ink on paper 40 x 30cm

Coming Home

When frightened by change
Serenity clings to my sleep
and wonders remain
Their world will inherit its meek
and wicked's the taste
You feel when the mysteries arise
I've fallen from grace
because of her treacherous eyes

You don't know, so alone

So alone, so alone, and thats why I'm coming home

And beauty's disdain
Attends to these virtuous lies
She tries to restrain
the ardent and amorous eyes
and wicked's the taste
you feel when mysteries arise
I've fallen from grace
because of her treacherous eyes

You don't know so alone

So alone, and that why I'm coming home

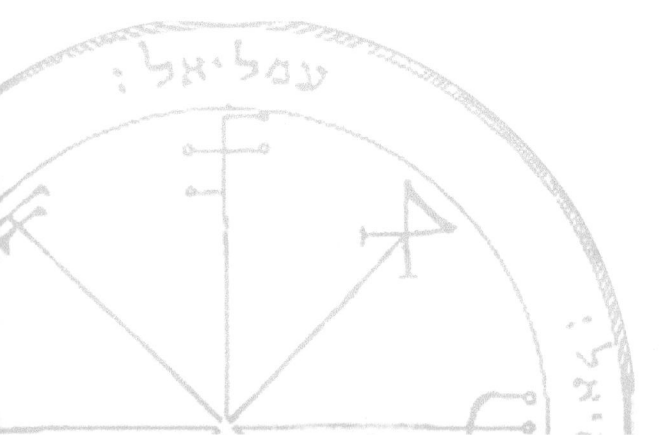

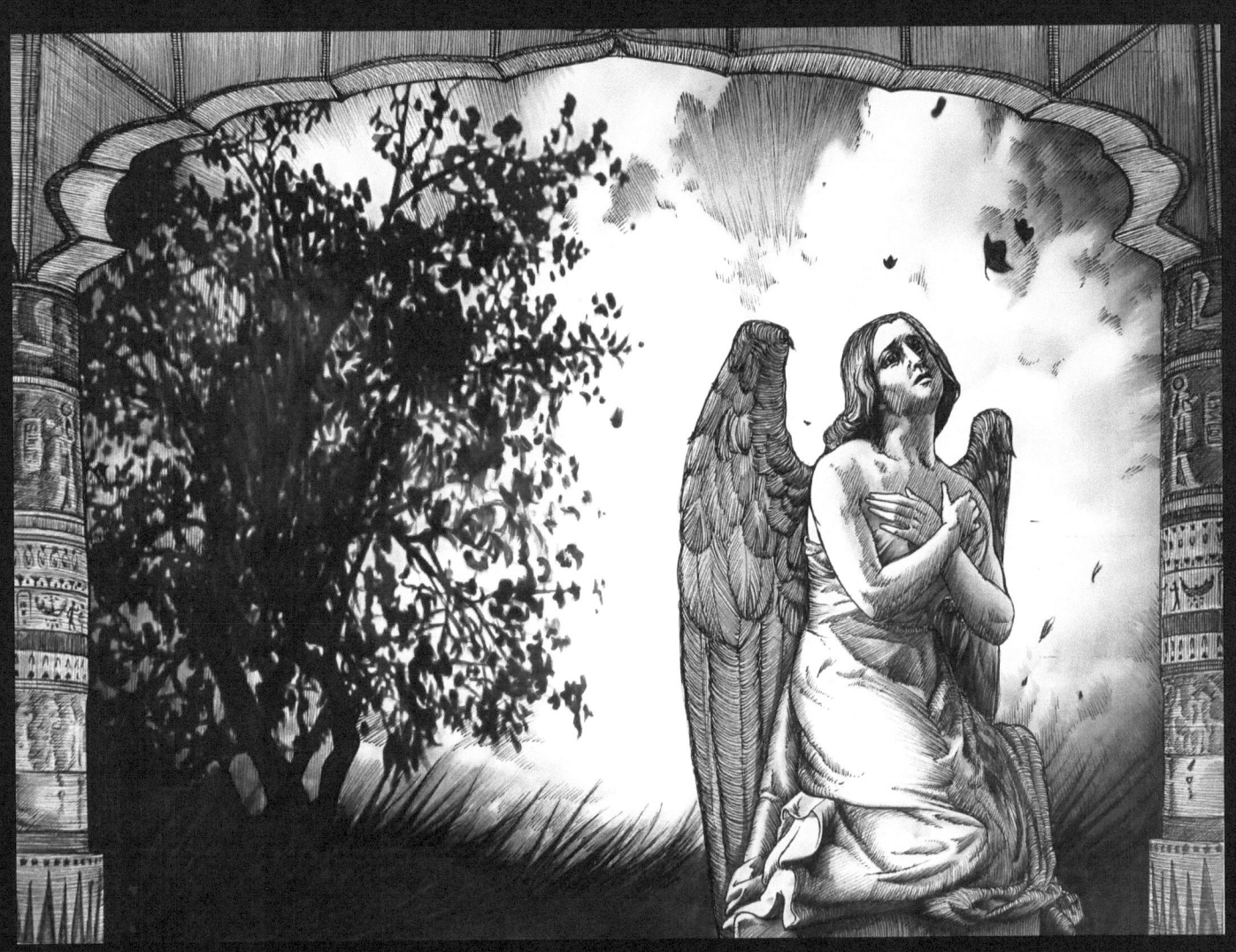

Coming Home   pen and ink on paper   40 x 30cm

to feel the warmth that's come undone
Do you sleep in sympathy
and if its true walk with me

All of the while you were here
All of the while you were near

In the twilight the idols speak
and in the twilight you'll always seek
A sentimental forgotten friend
who will always love you until the end

All of the while you were here
All of the while you were near

And now you search for the ideals
you'll find a vice that always heals
the open wounds, the bleeding hearts
yet still they'll say you're torn apart

All of the while you were here
All of the while you were near

Come on lady walk with me
Come on lady talk with me
Can't you see I'm all alone
This loneliness I can't condone
Come on lady hold my hand
Take me to your shadowland
Sleep awhile in sympathy
Come on lady walk with me

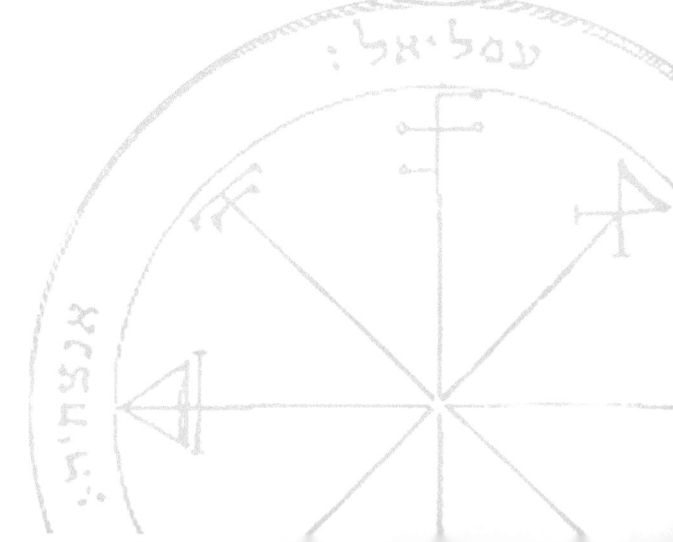

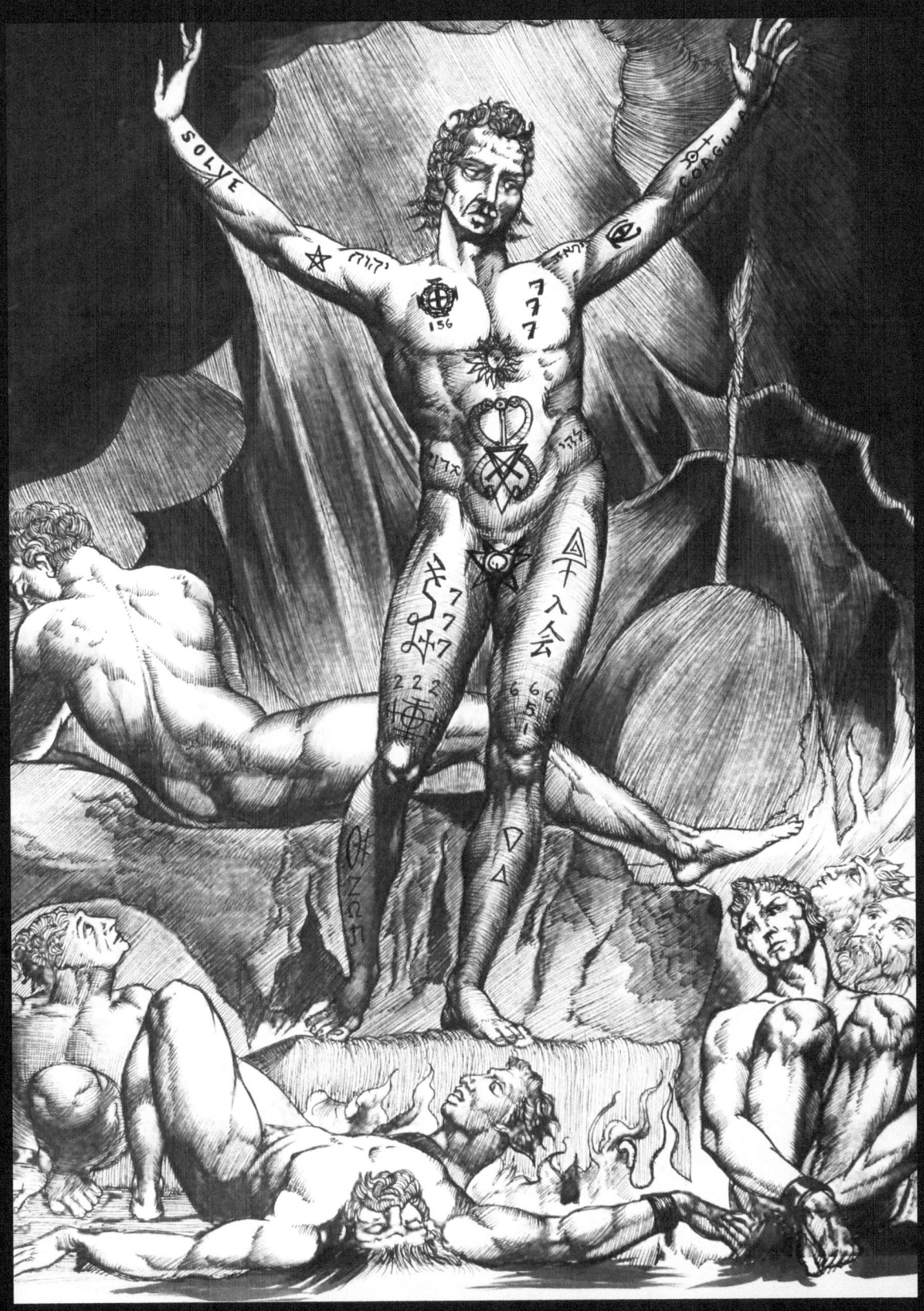

Walk with Me   pen and ink on paper   40 x 30cm

Film Collection

Selected stills from "The Edges of Twilight"
A series of 12 short films exhibited in Canada and Australia
August - November 2015

All films created by Robert Buratti

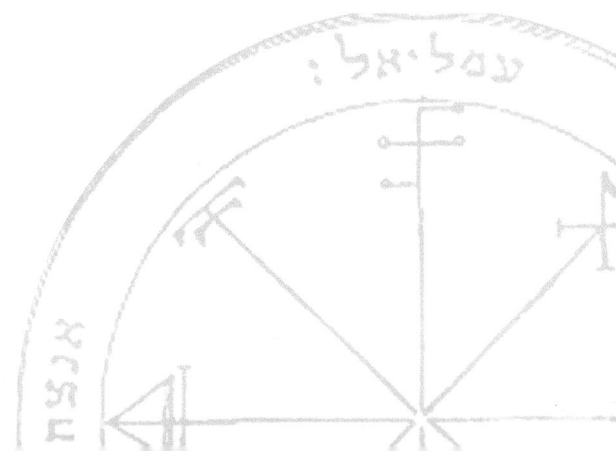

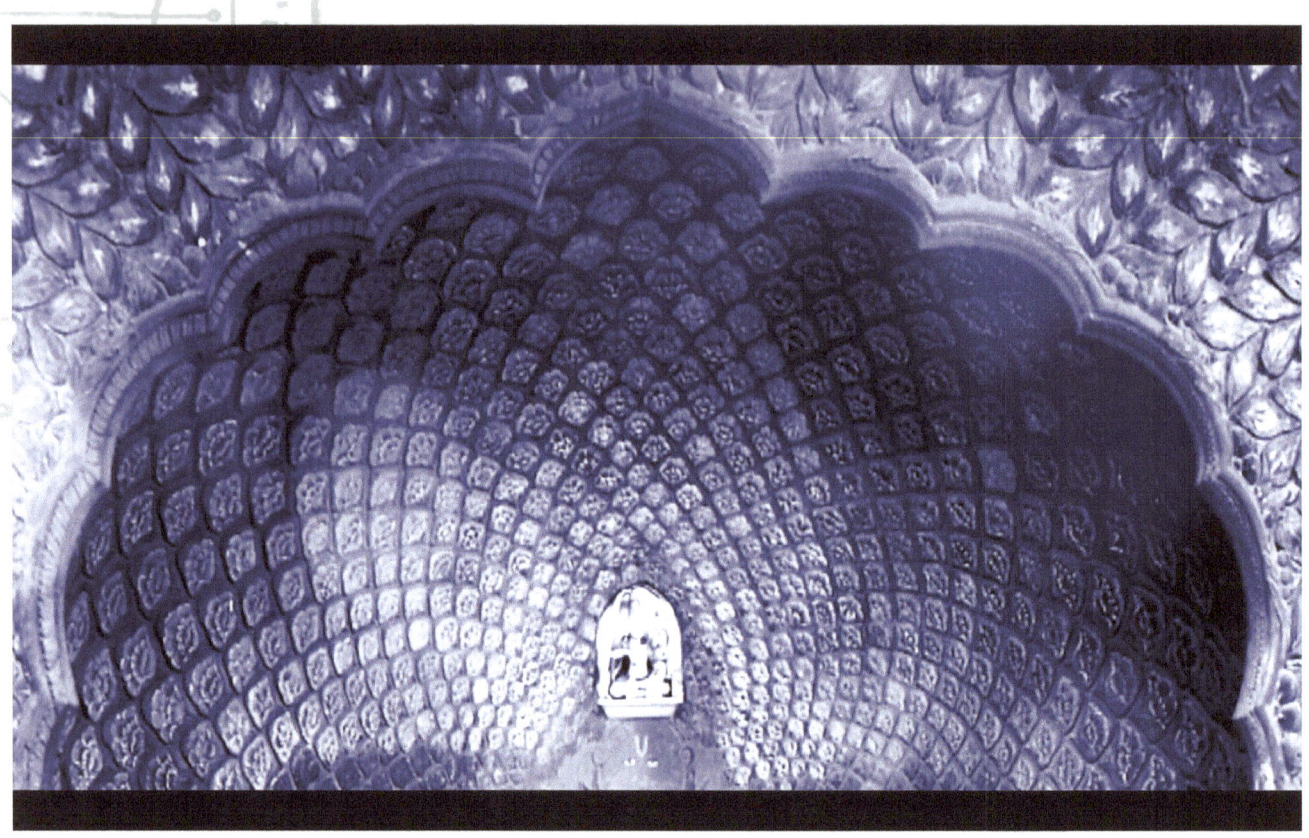

Fire in the Head short film 5.06 minutes

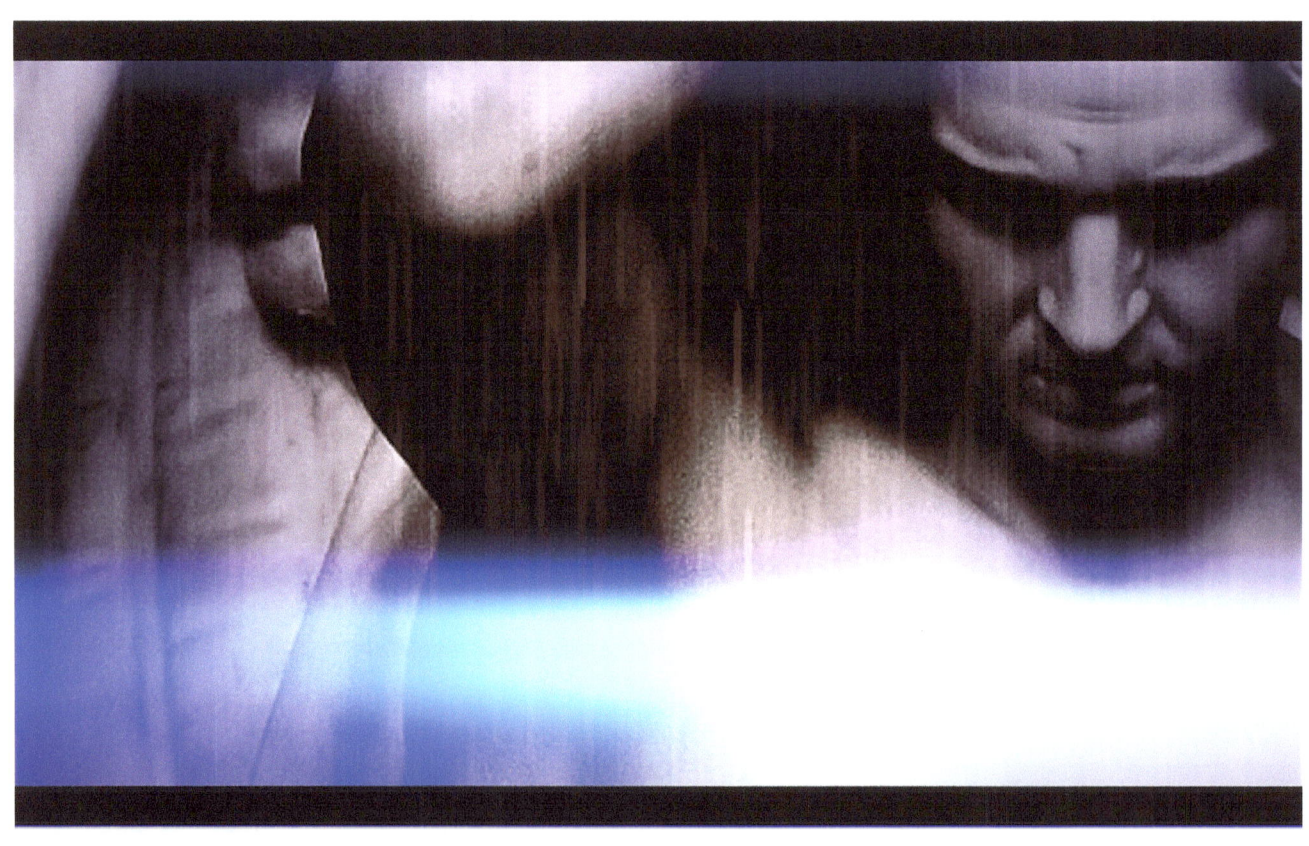

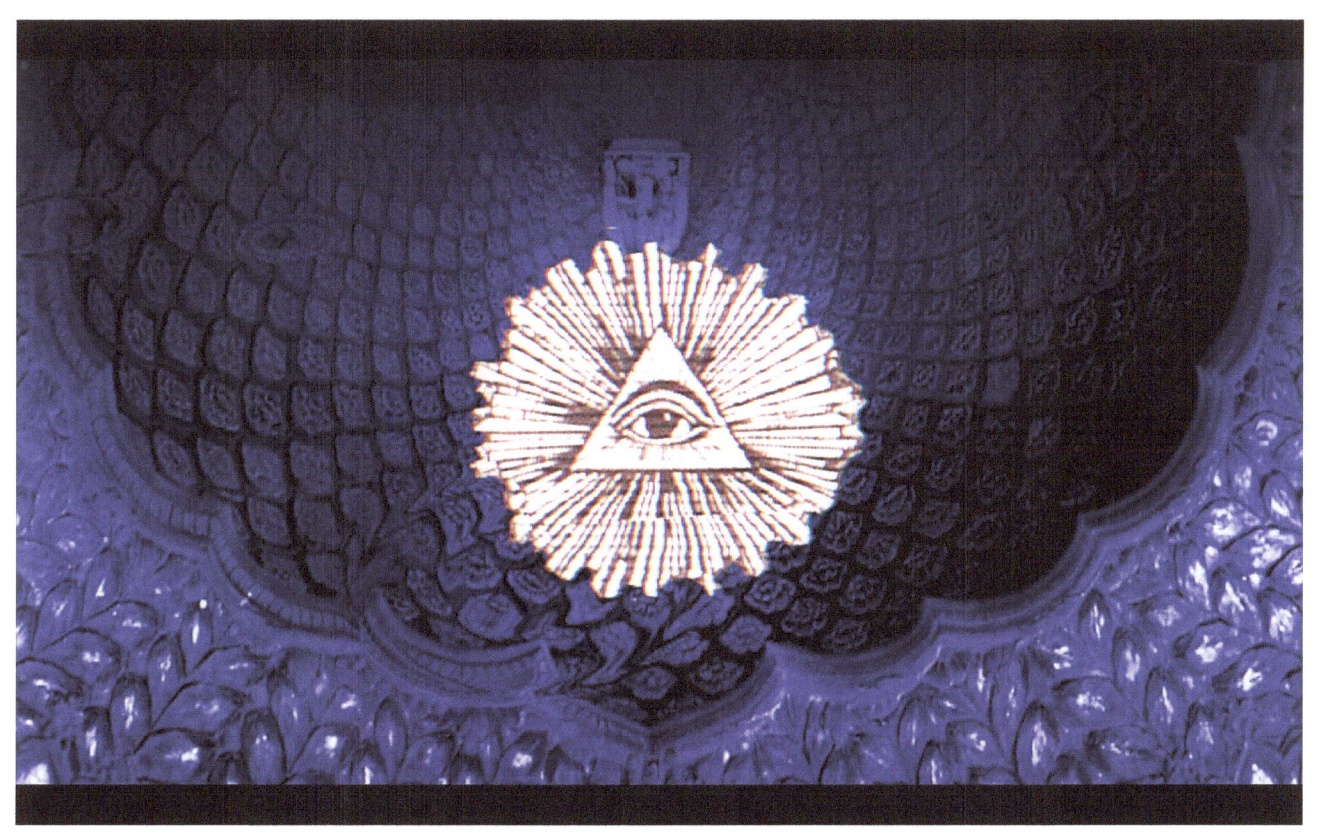

Fire in the Head short film 5.06 minutes

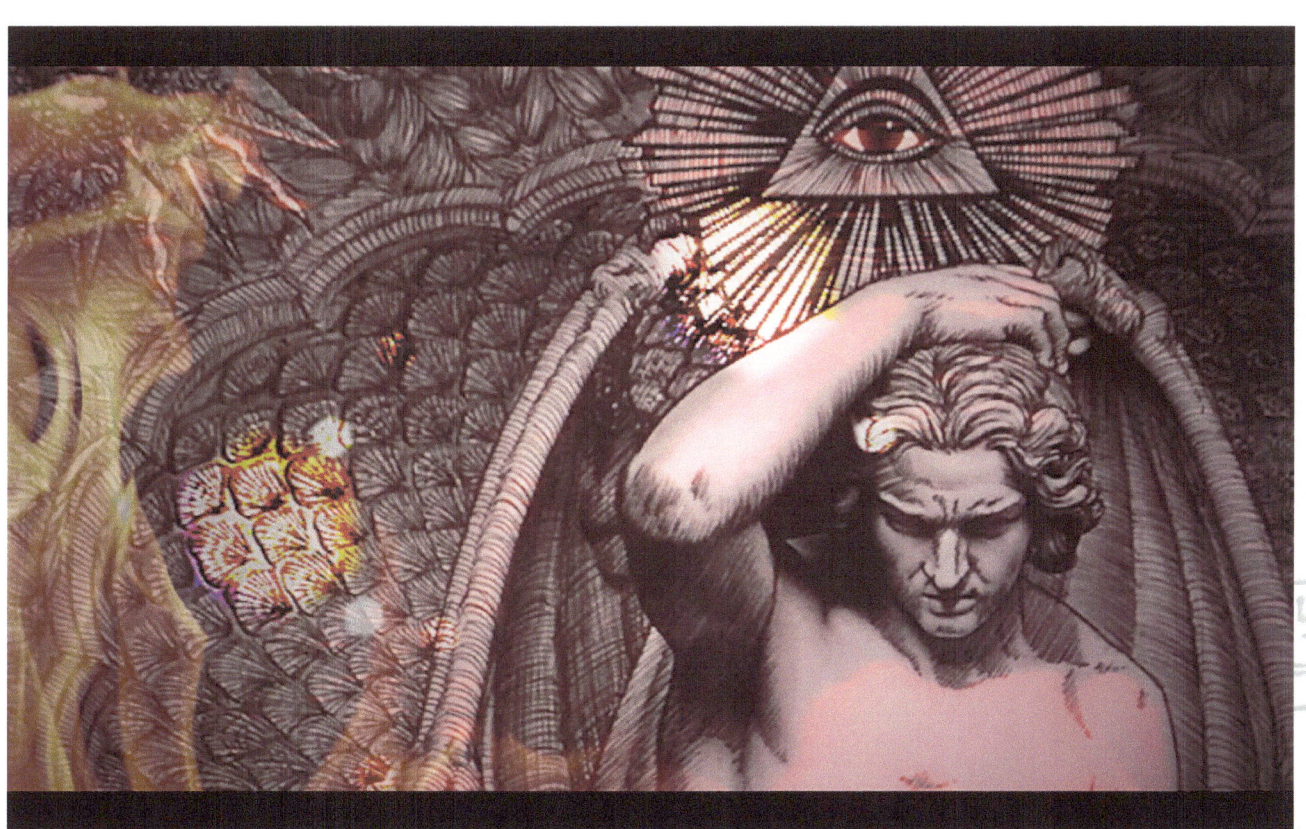

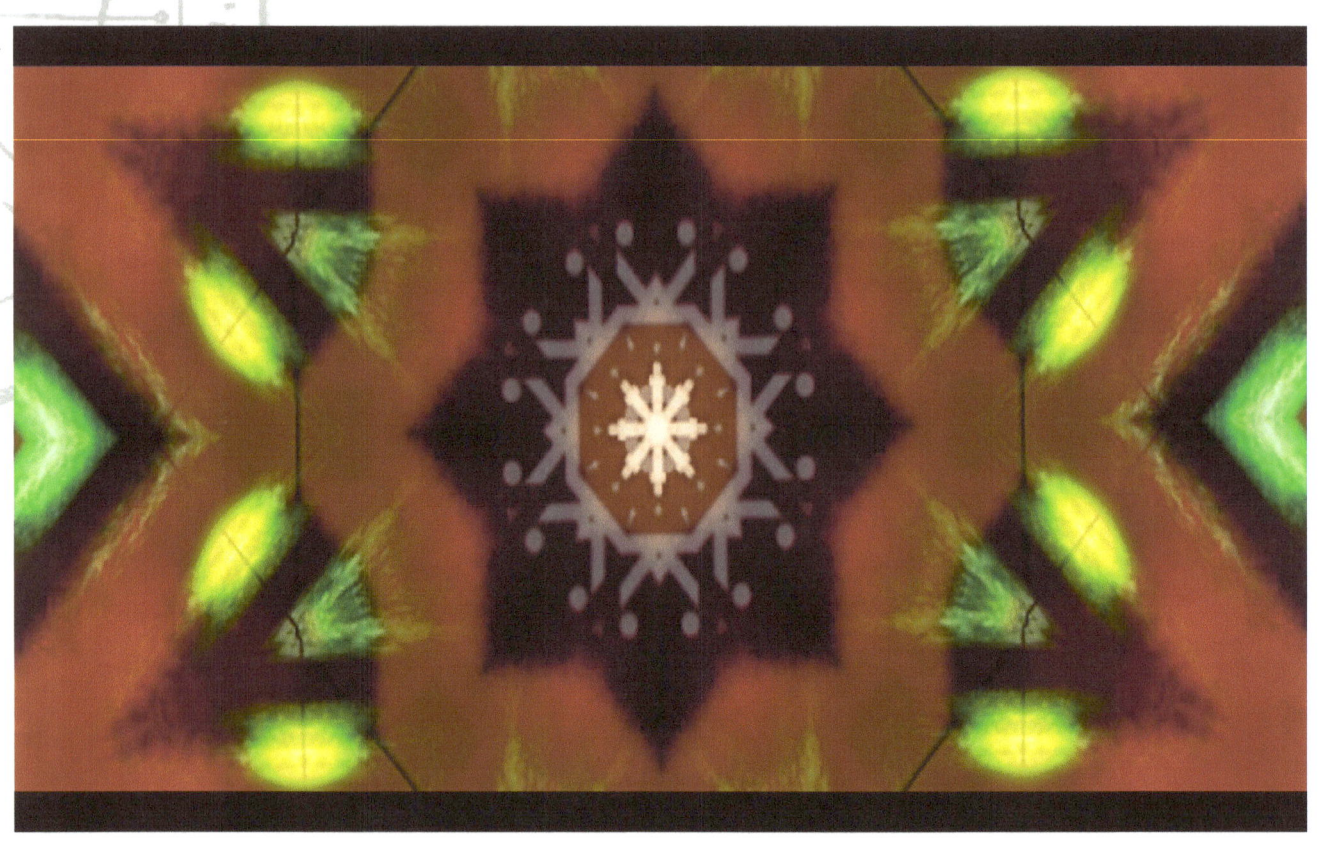

The Bazaar   short film 3.42 minutes

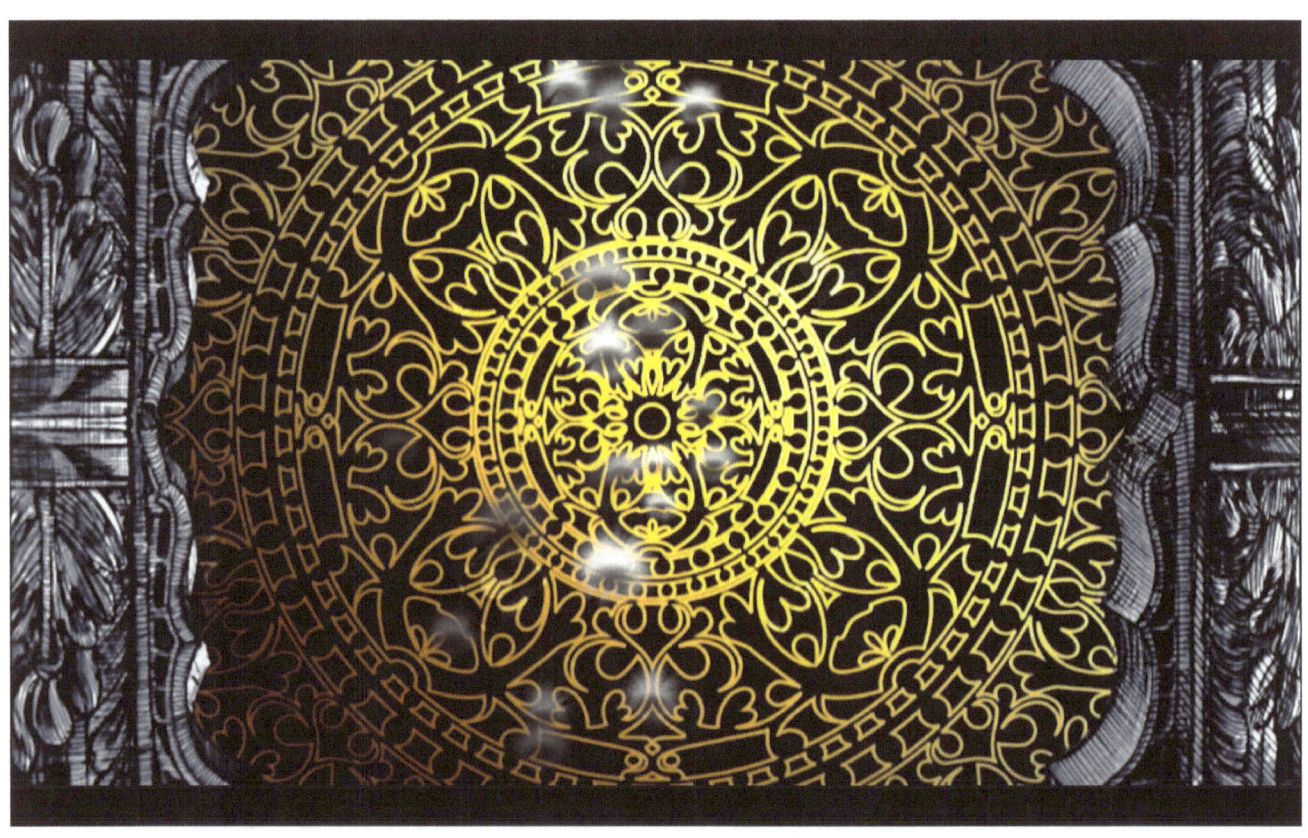

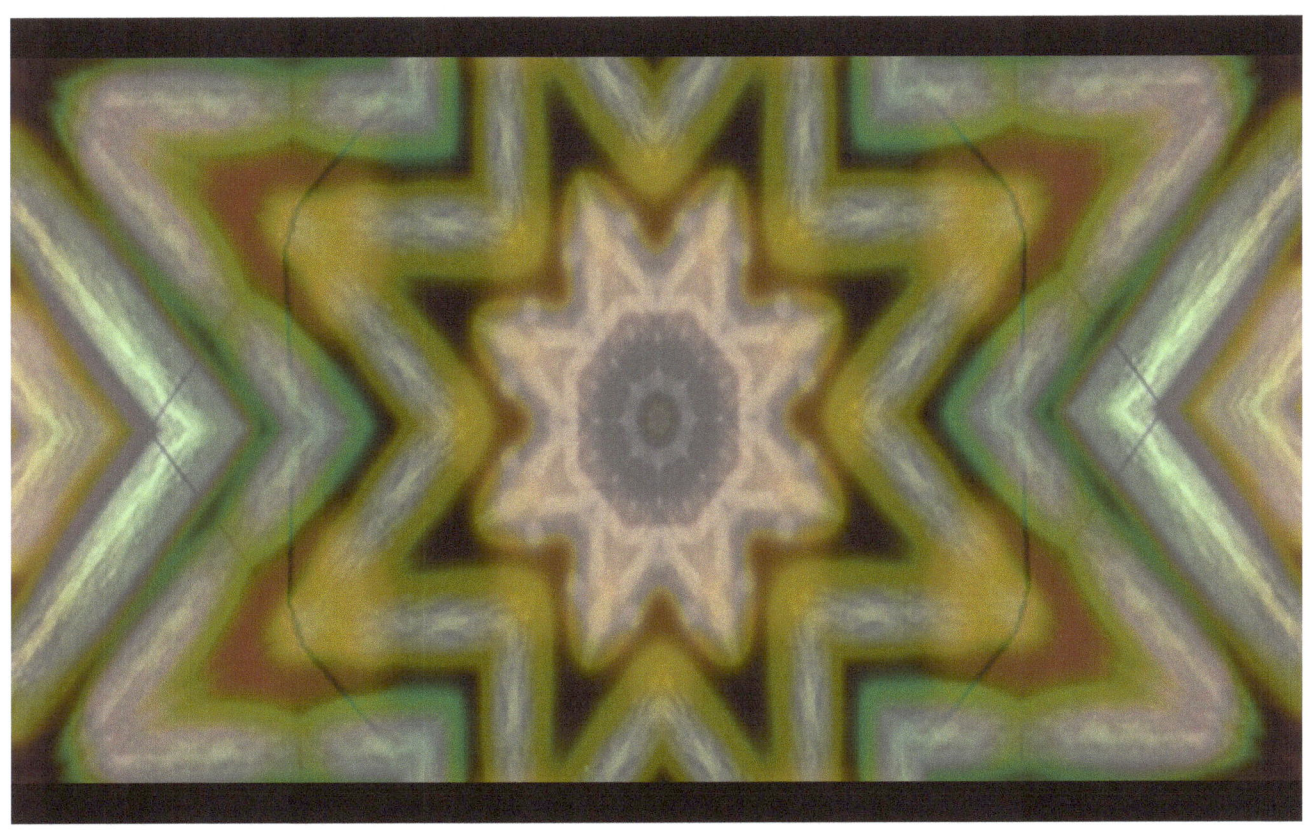

The Bazaar   short film 3.42 minutes

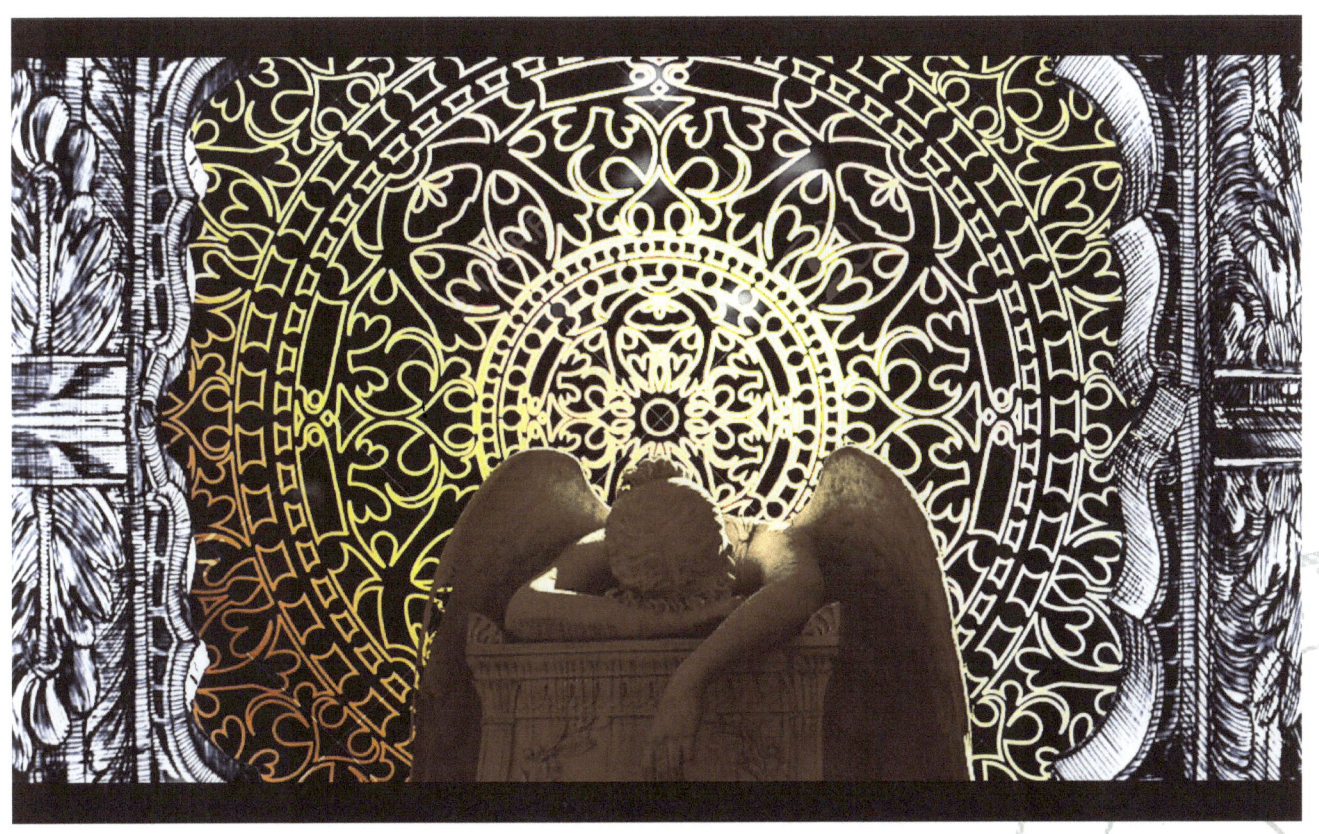

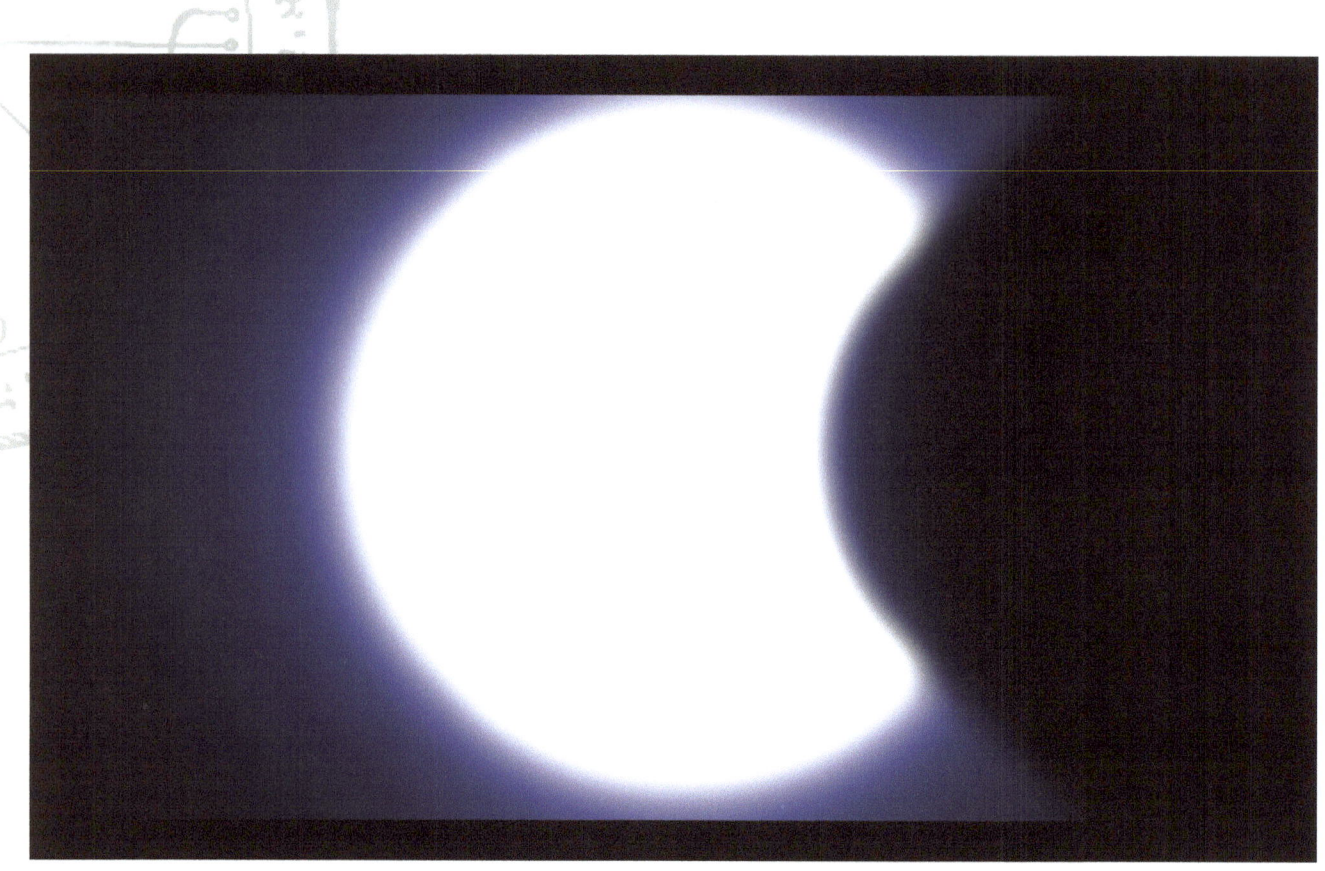

Correspondences   short film   11.31 minutes

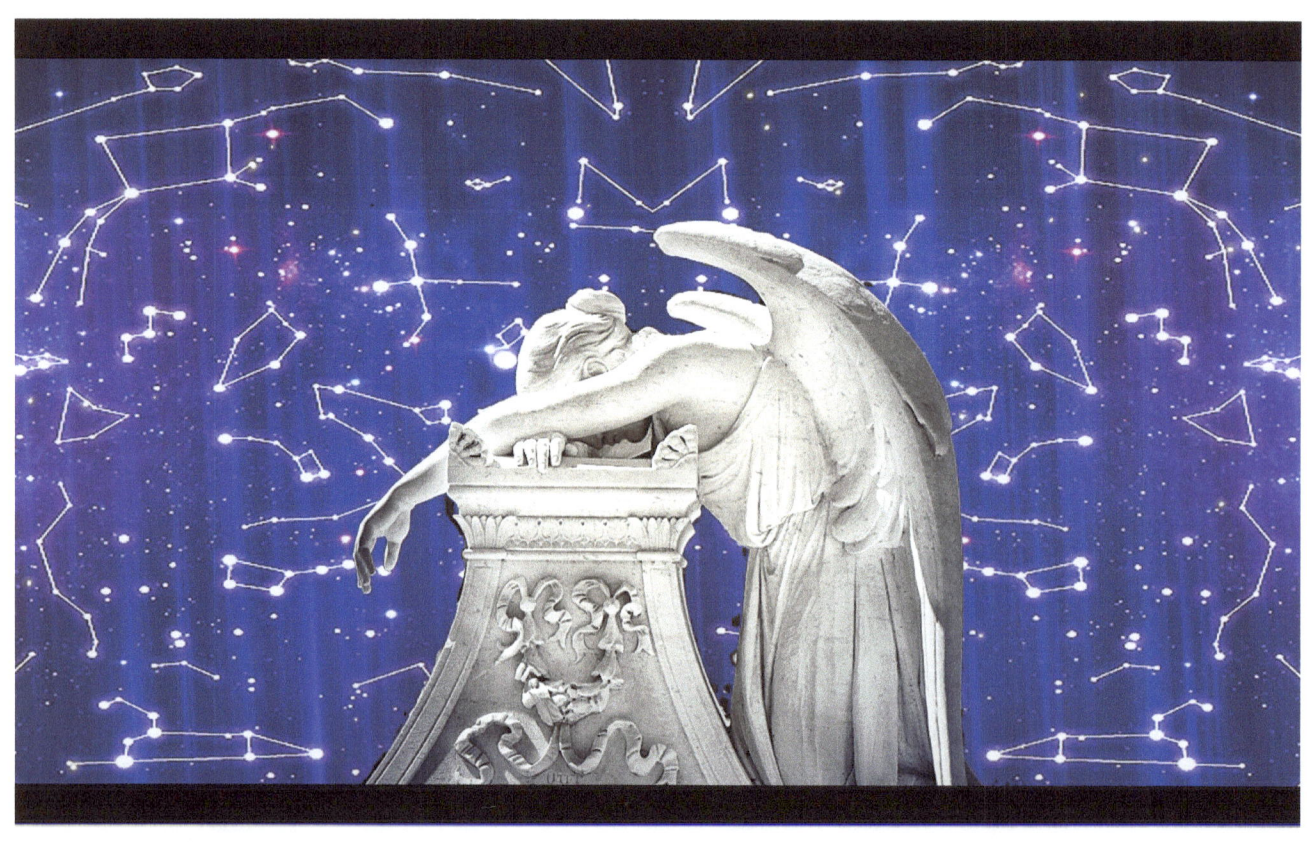

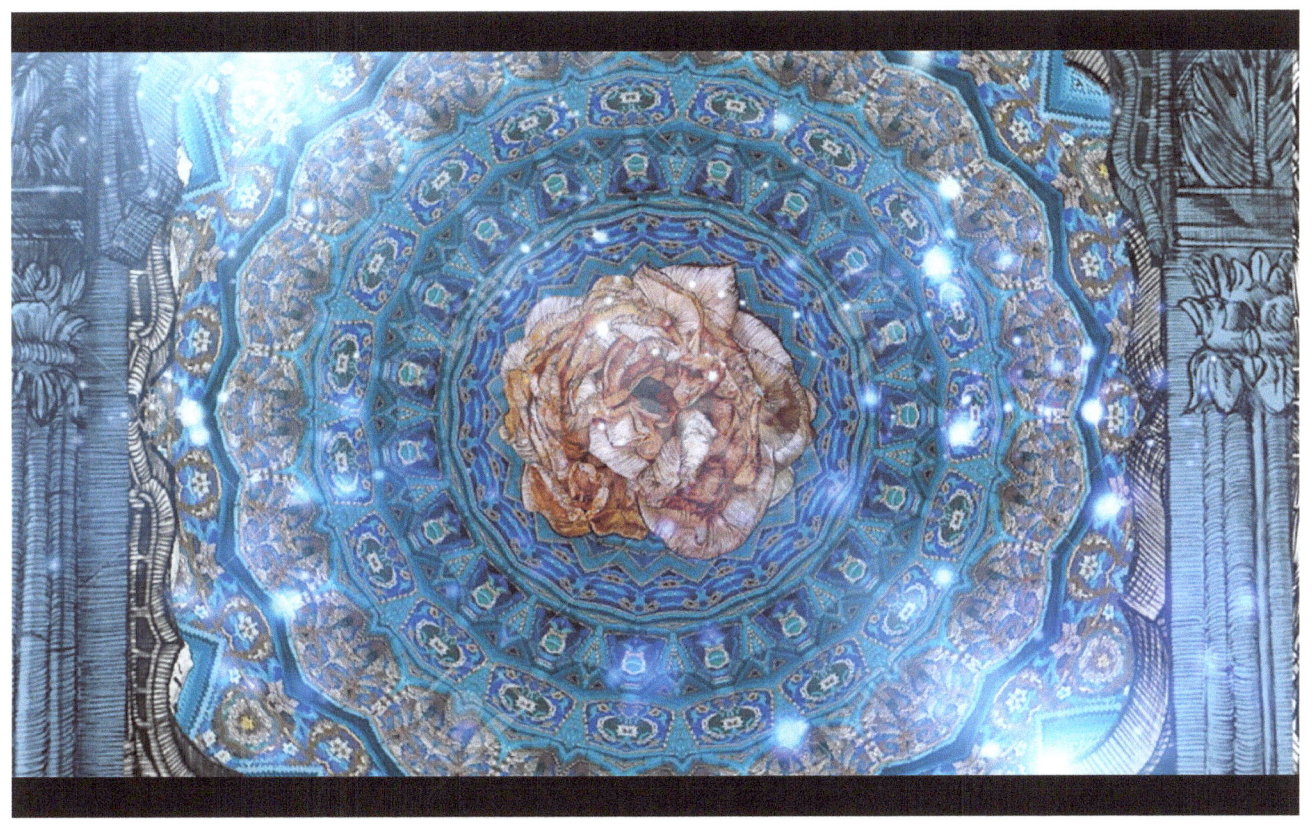

Silence short film 2.52 minutes

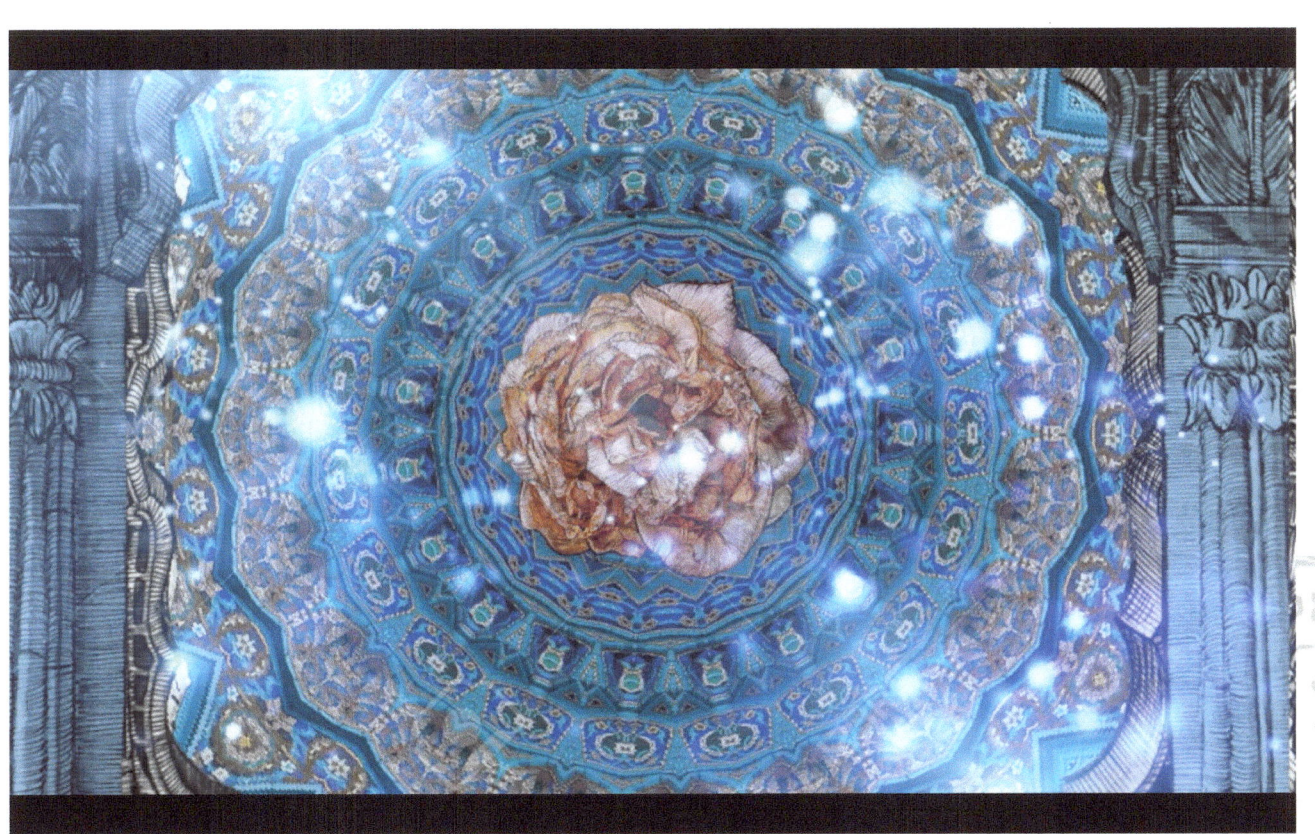

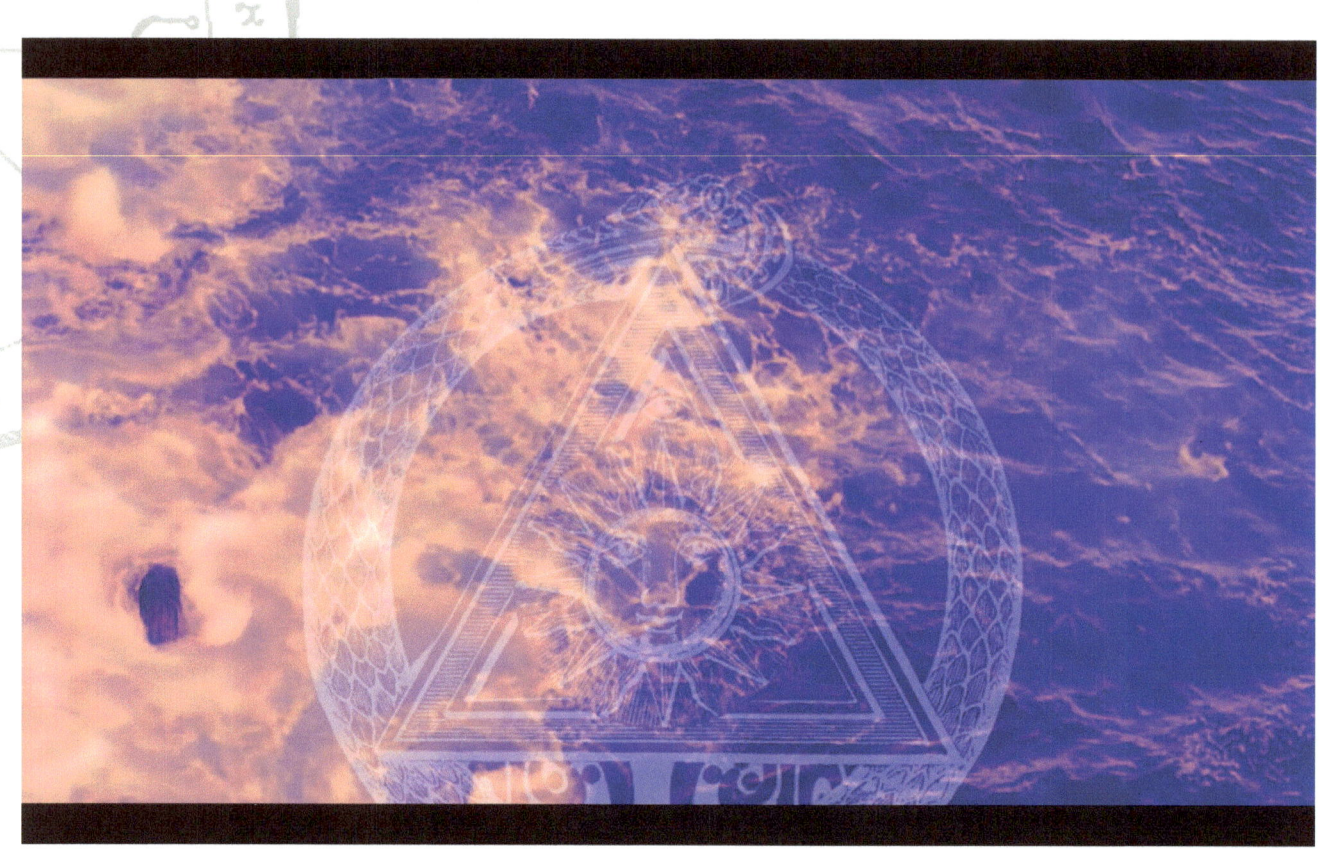

The Badger short film 3.59 minutes

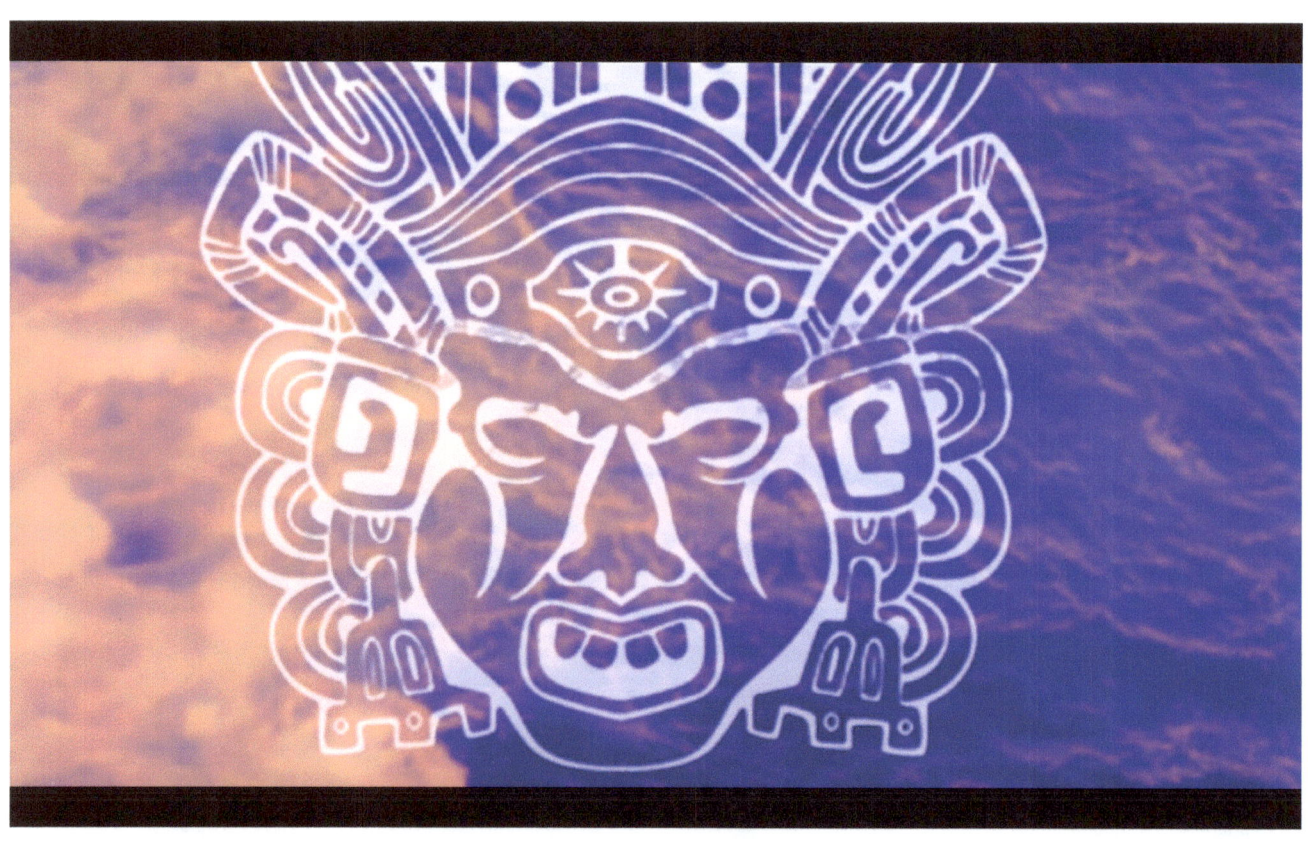

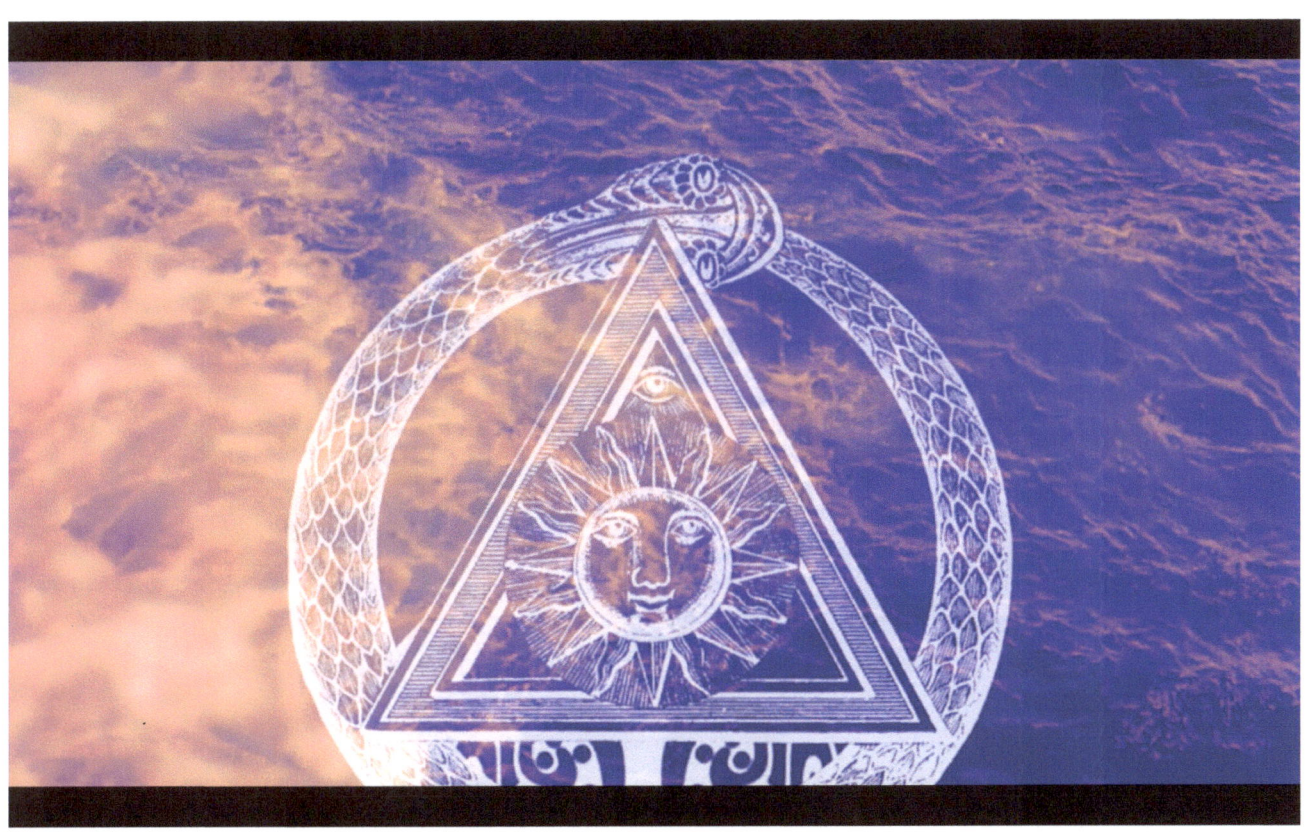

The Badger   short film 3.59 minutes

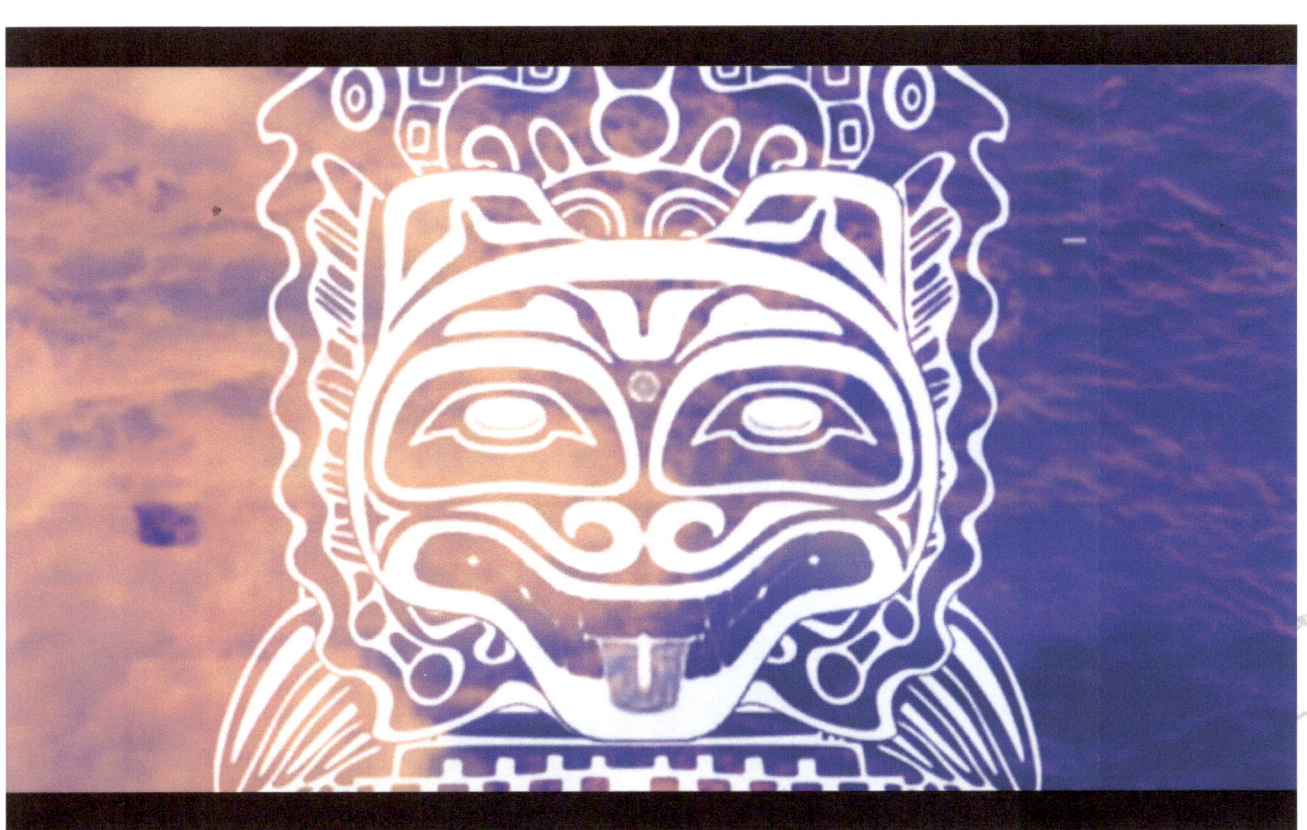

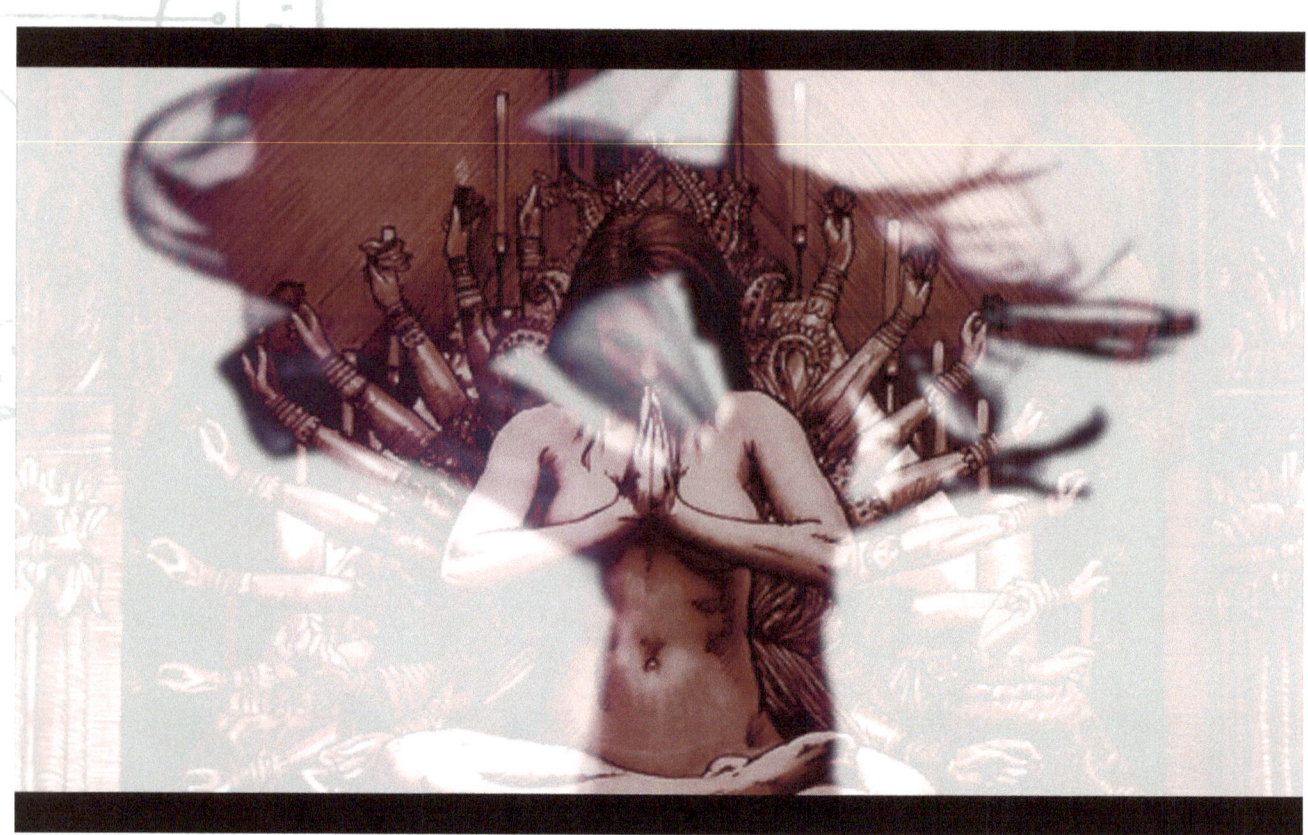

Sister Awake   short film 11 minutes

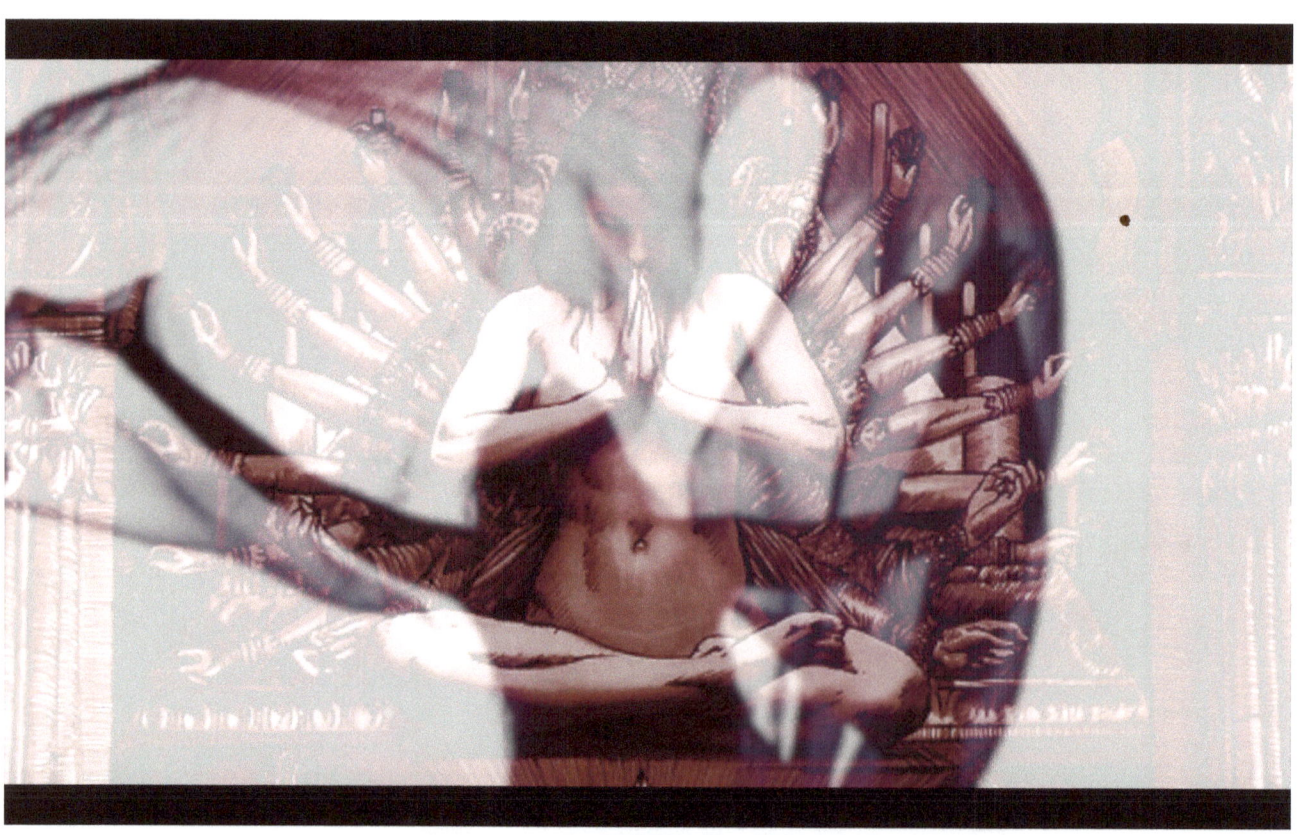

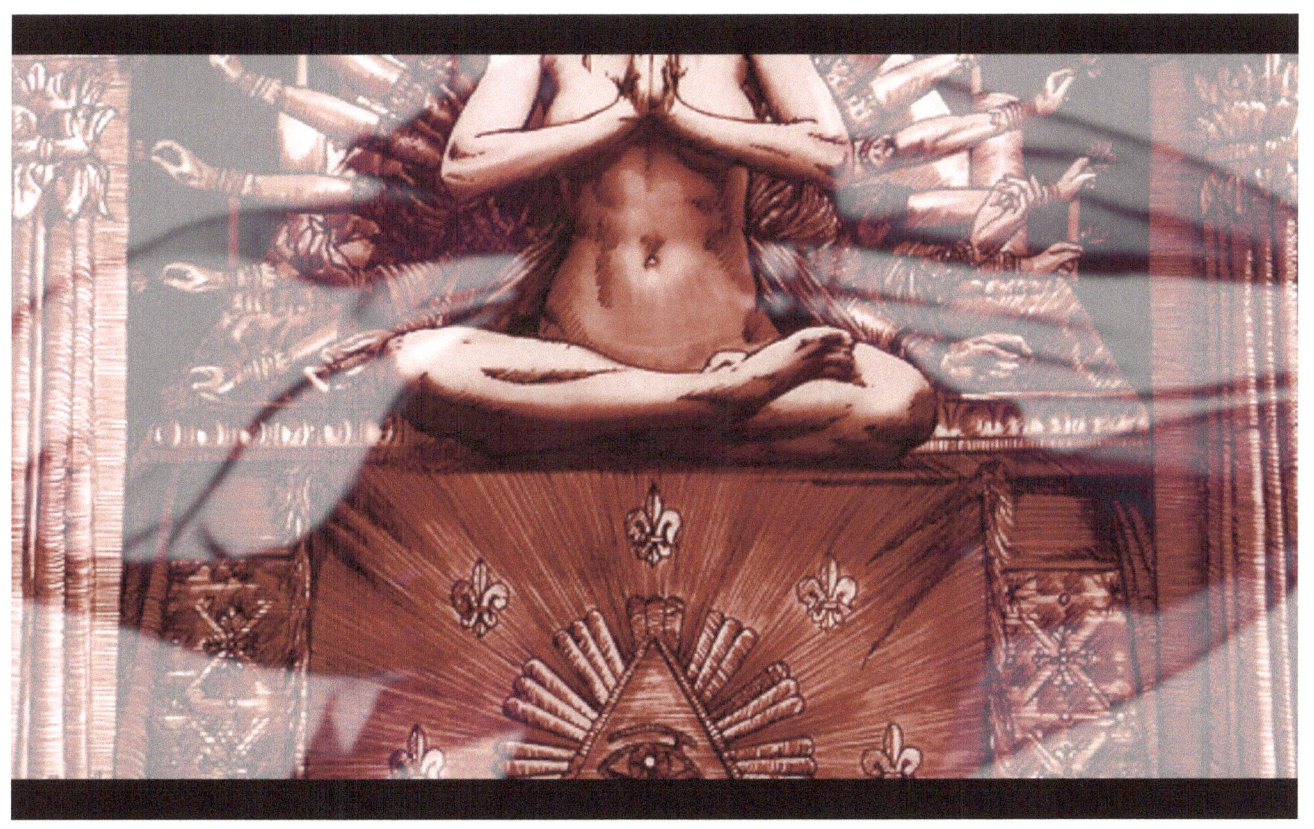

Sister Awake short film 11 minutes

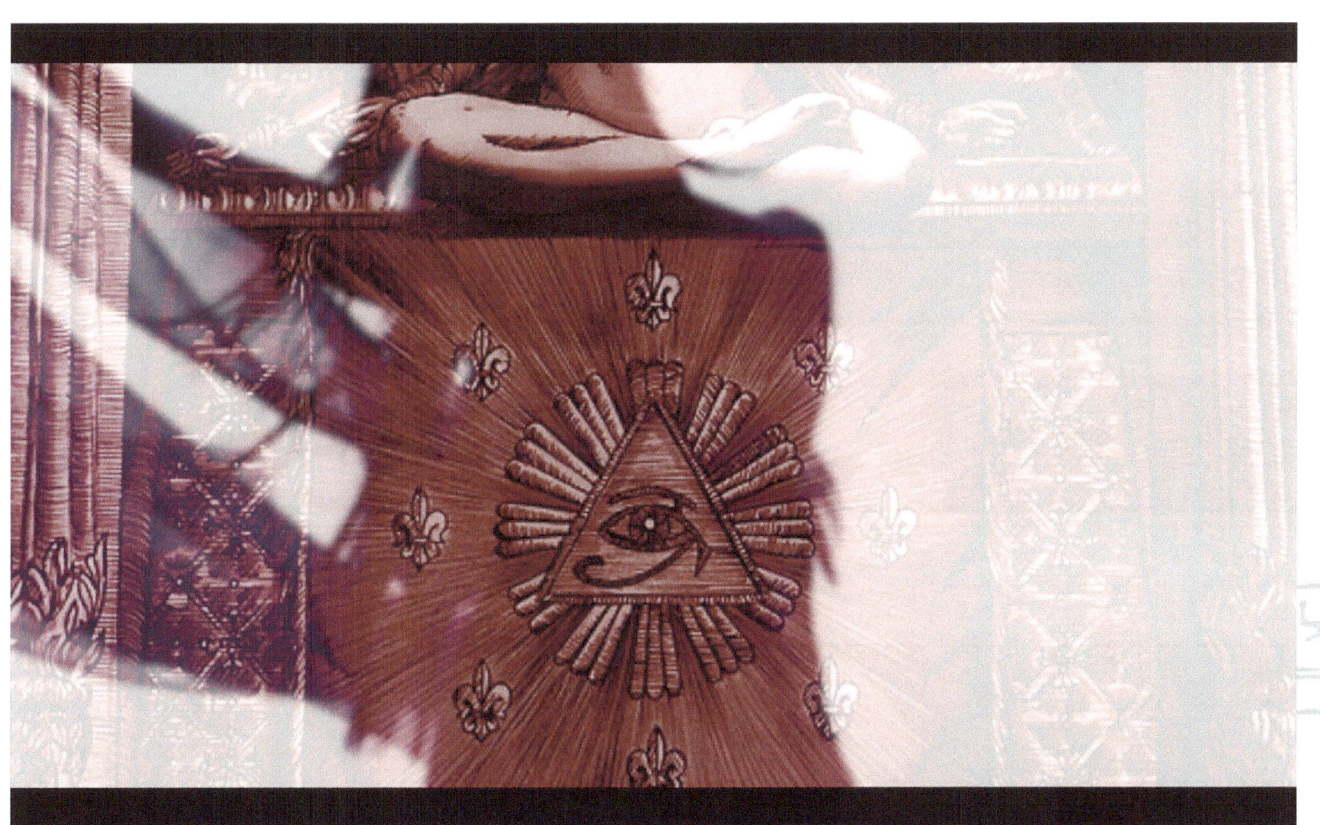

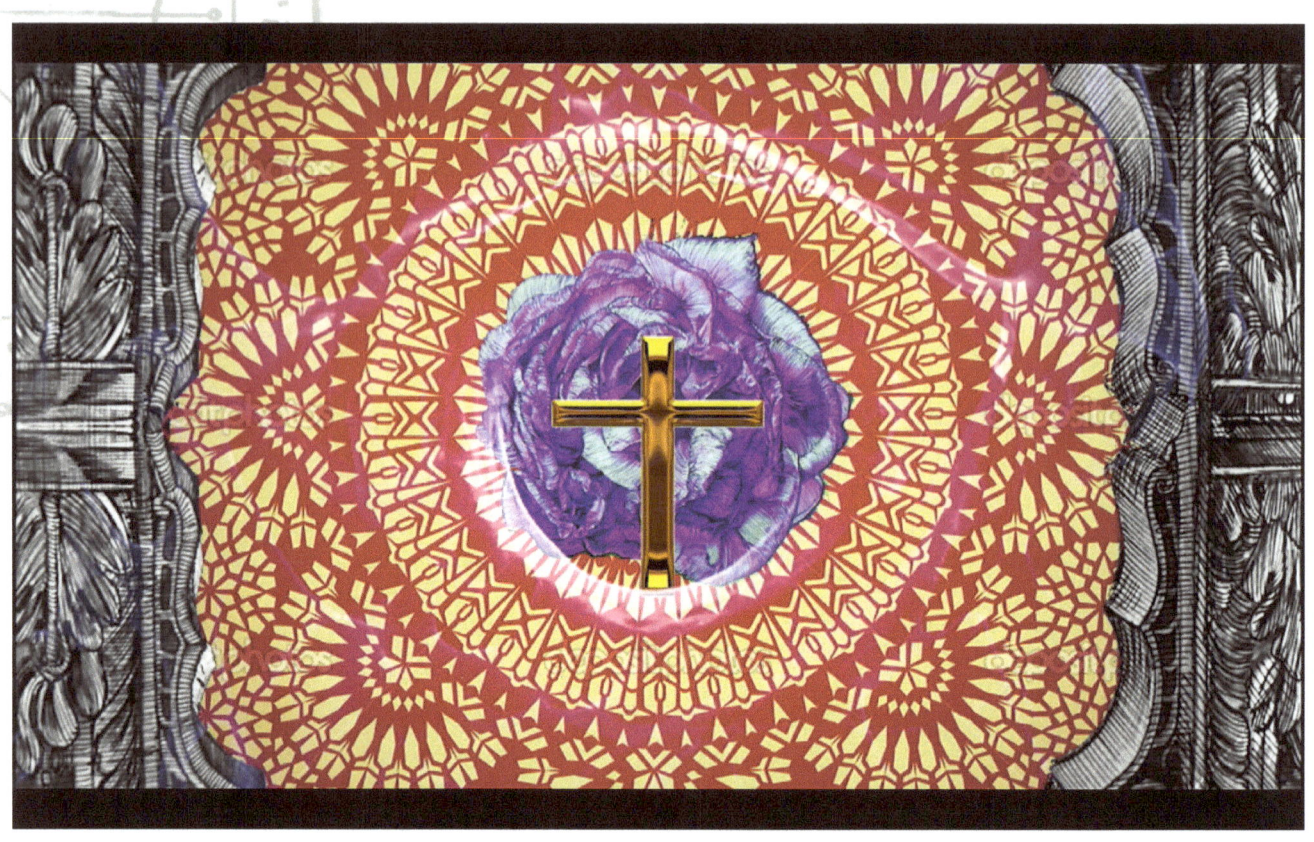

Turn the Lamp Down Low short film 5.17 minutes

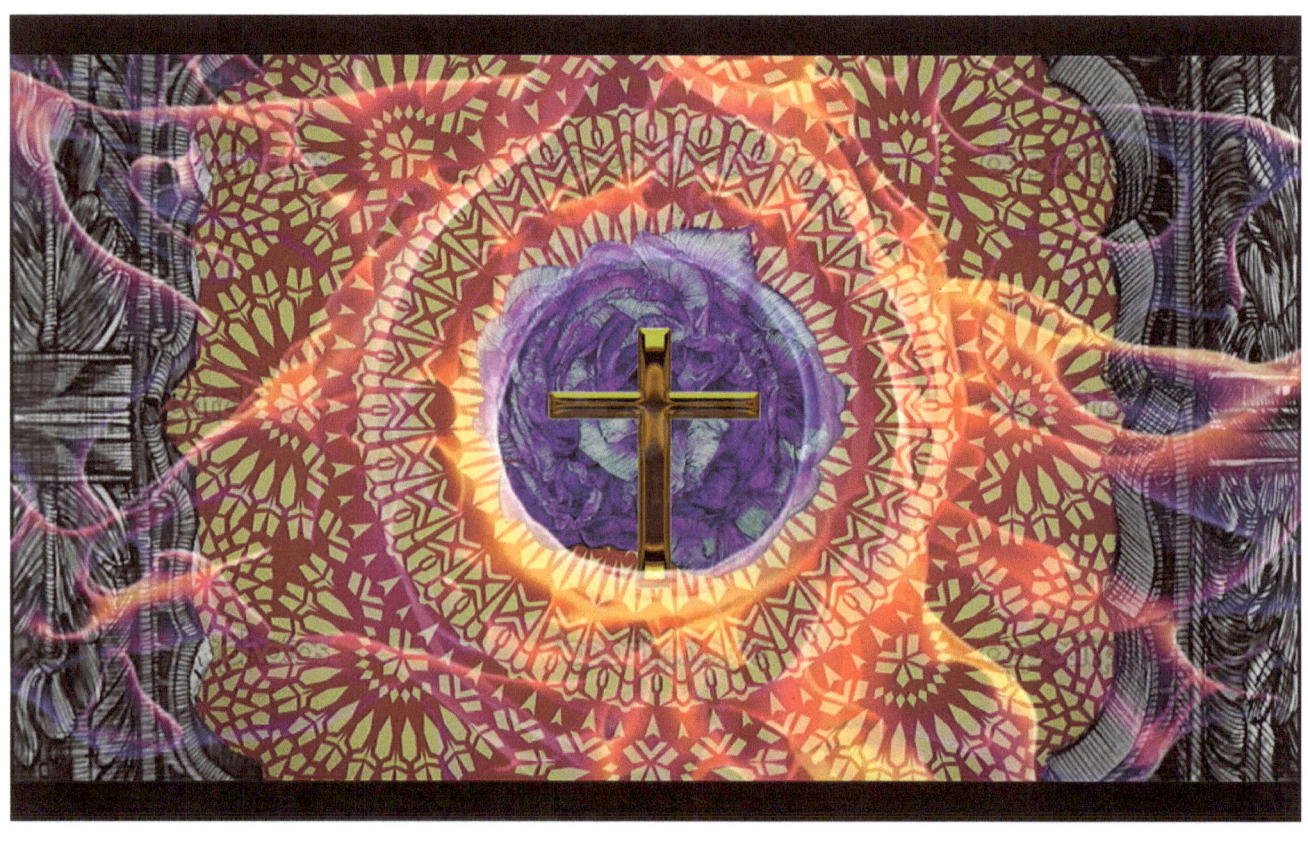

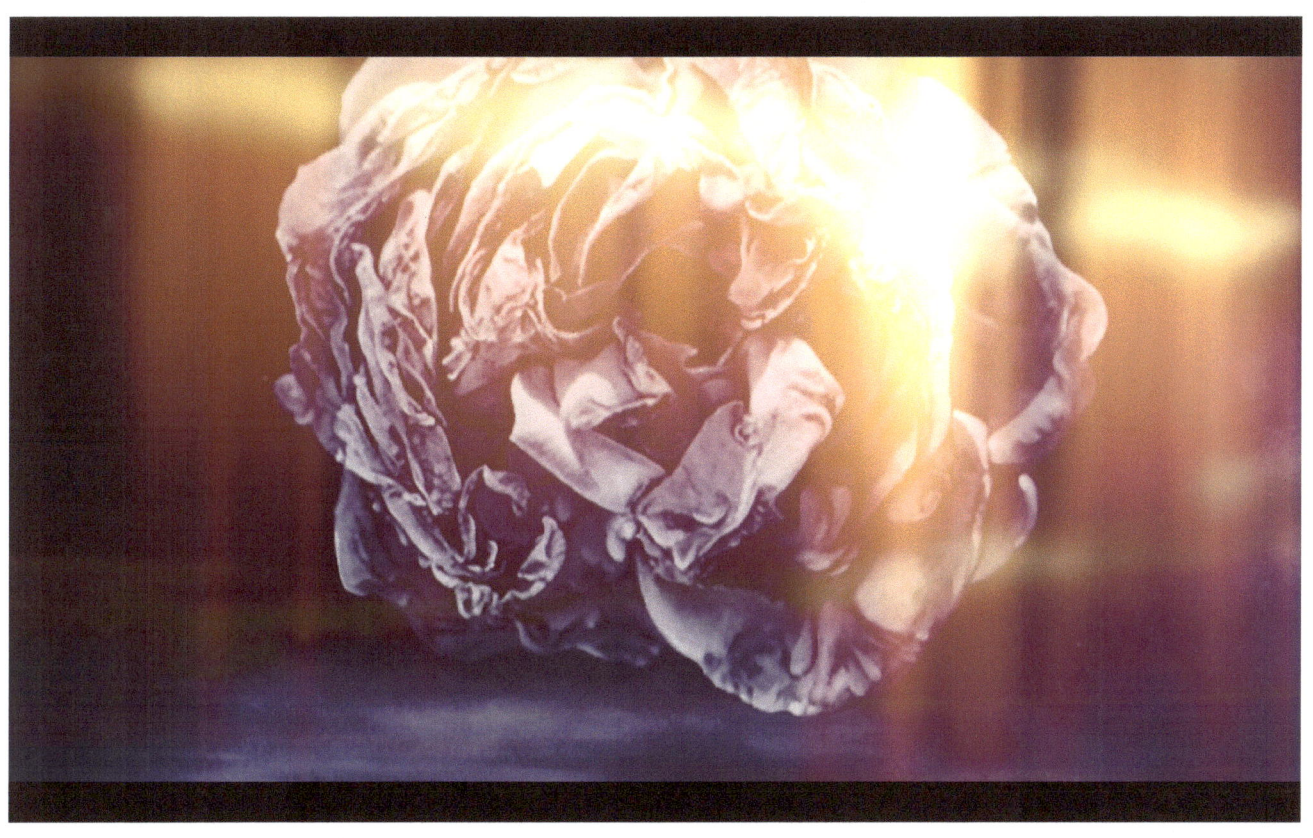

Shadows on the Mountainside   short film 3.40 minutes

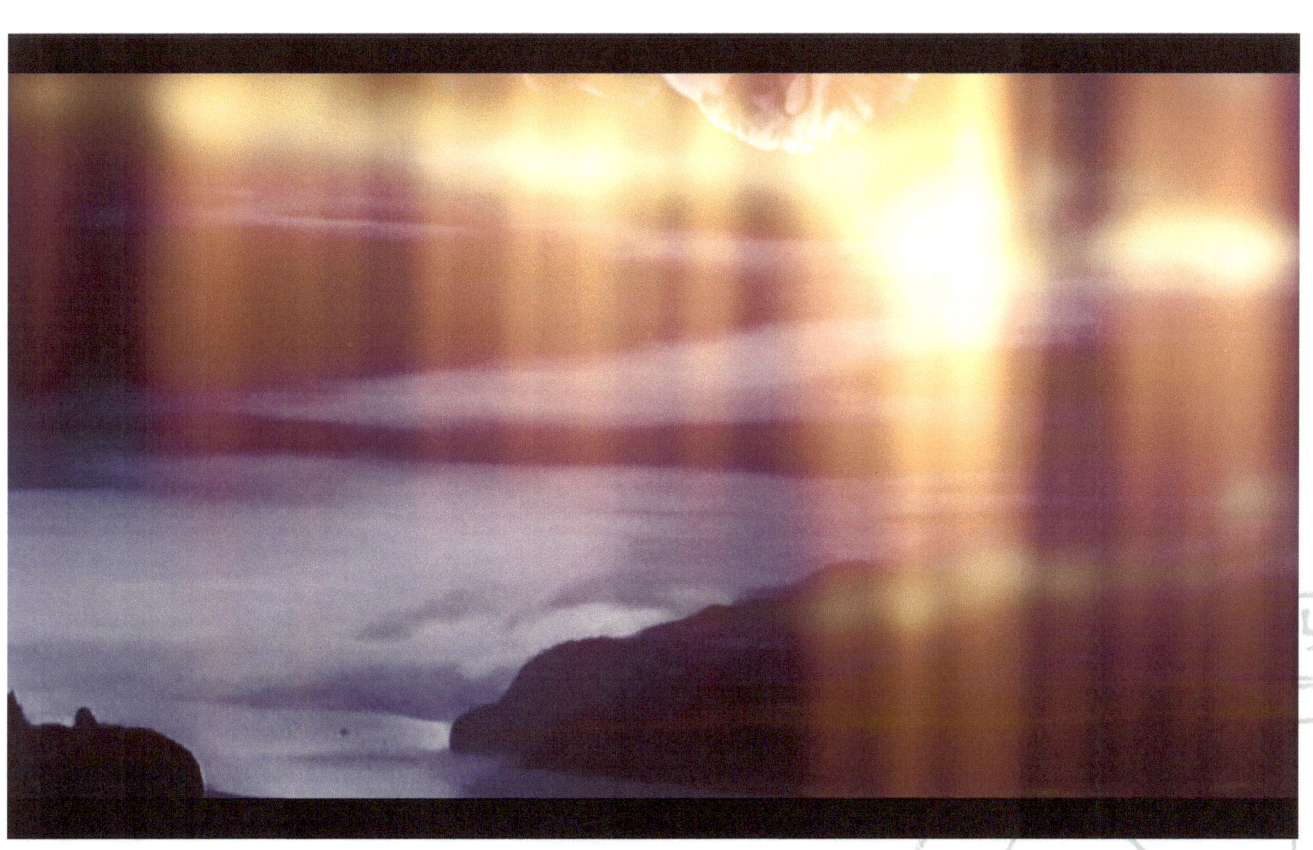

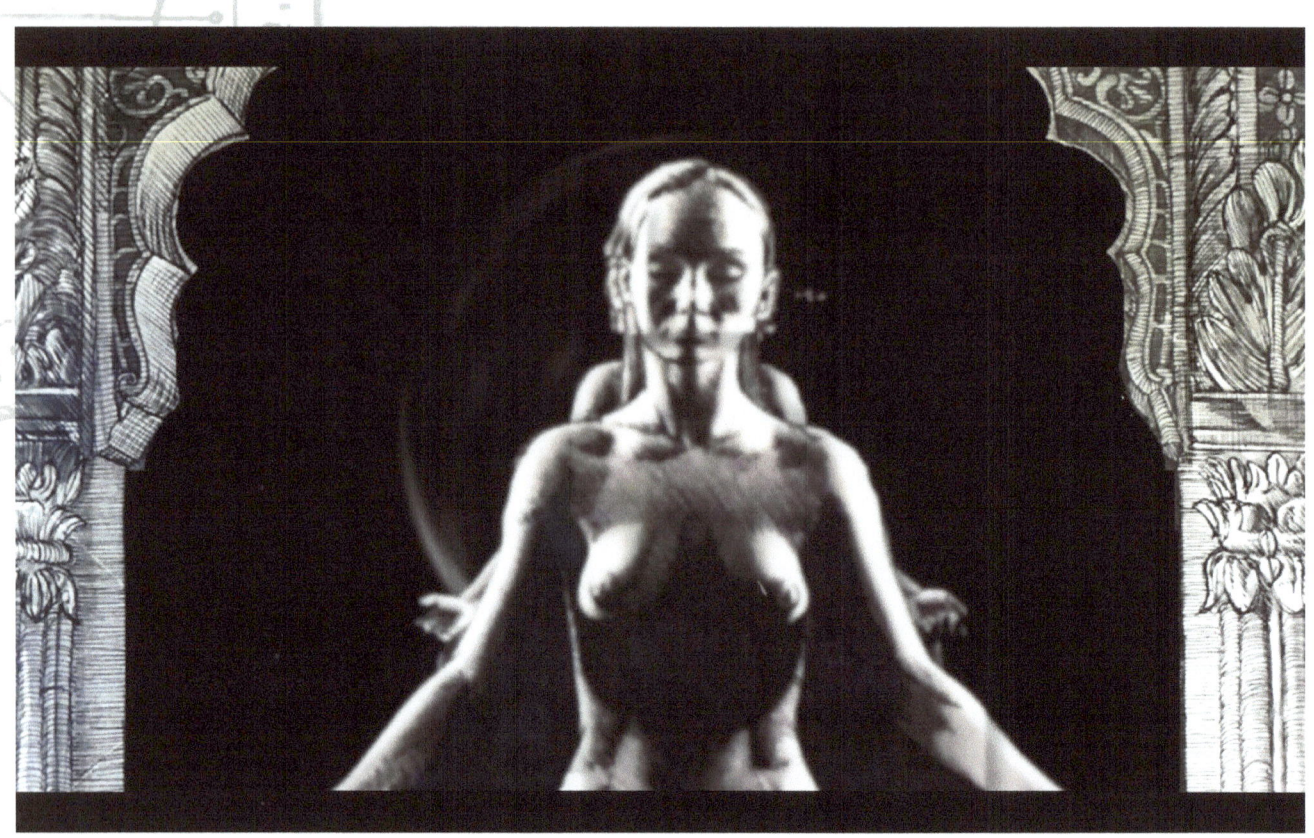

Drawing down the Moon short film 6.23 minutes

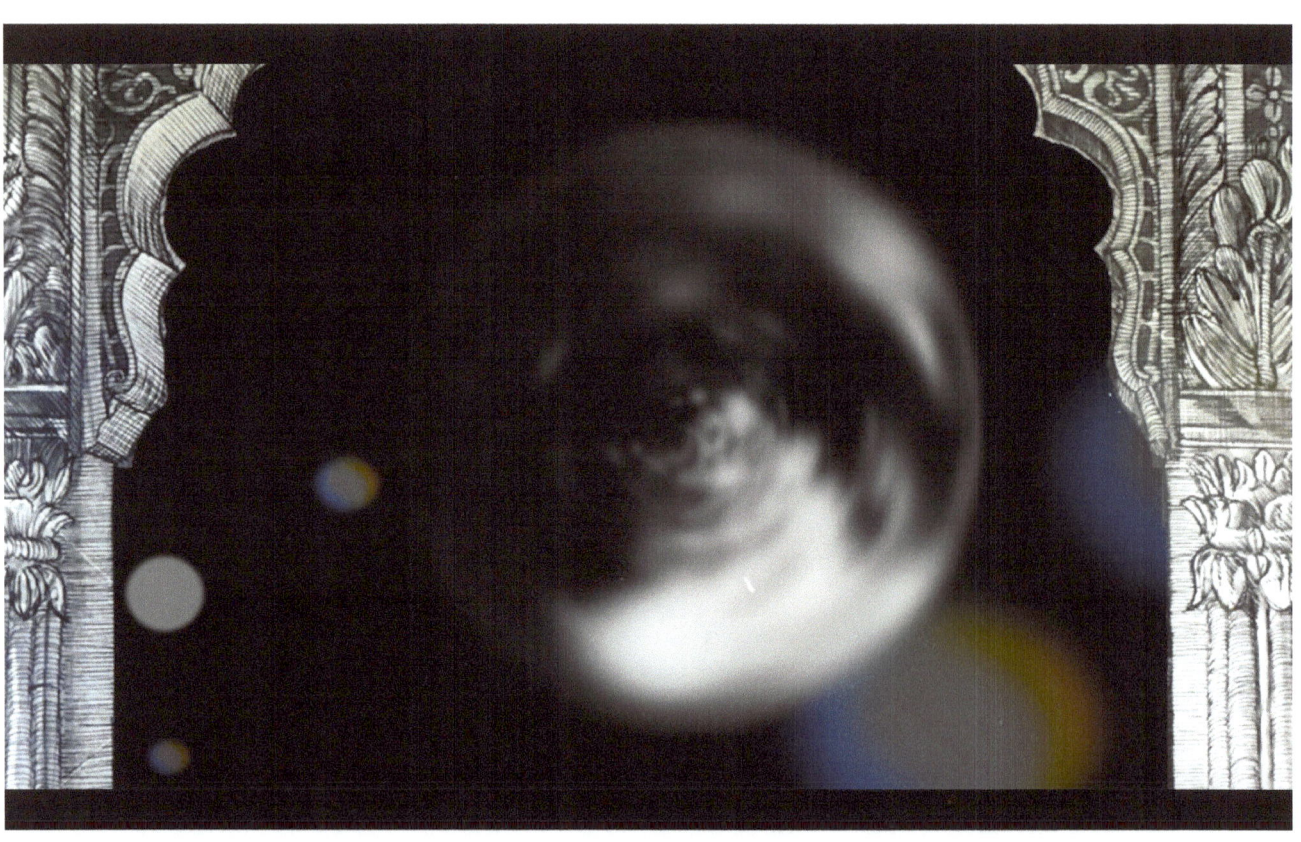

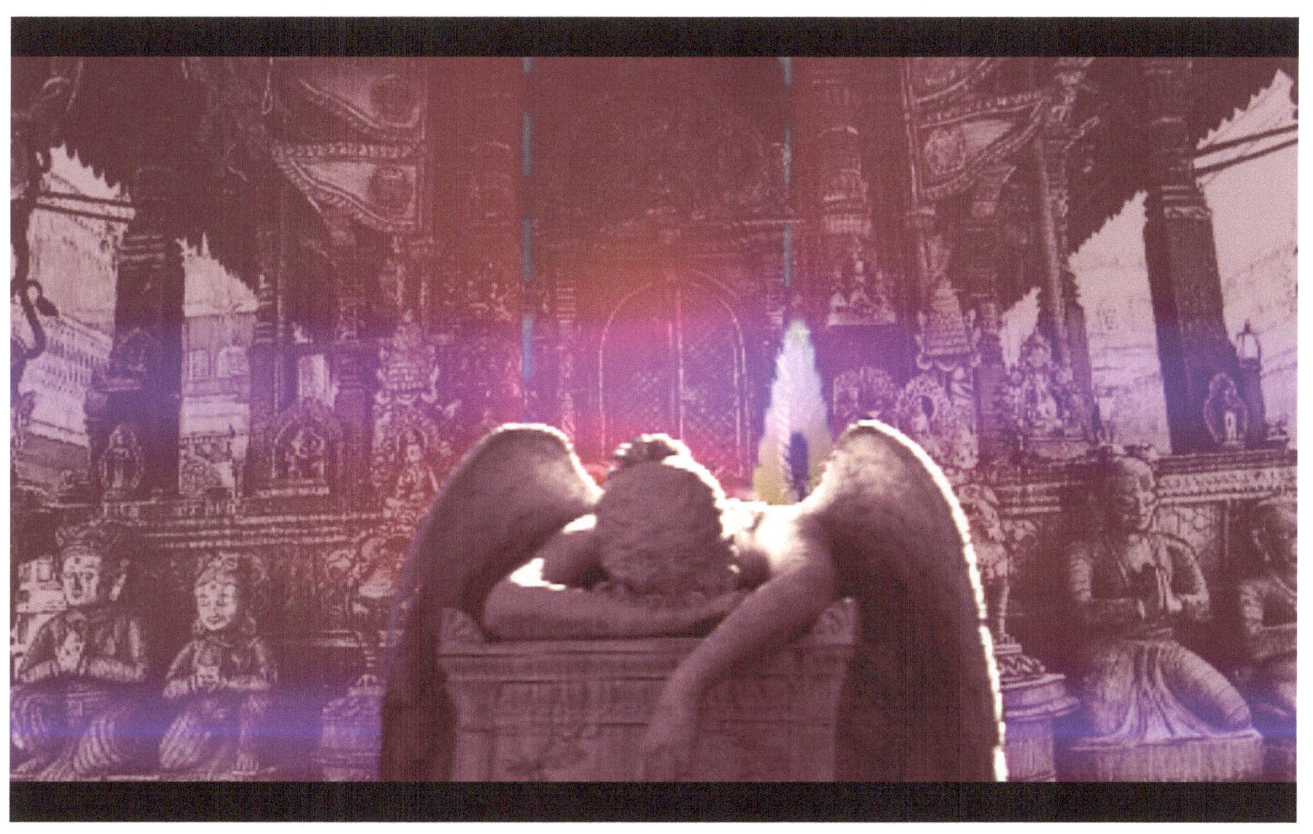

Inanna short film 3.49 minutes

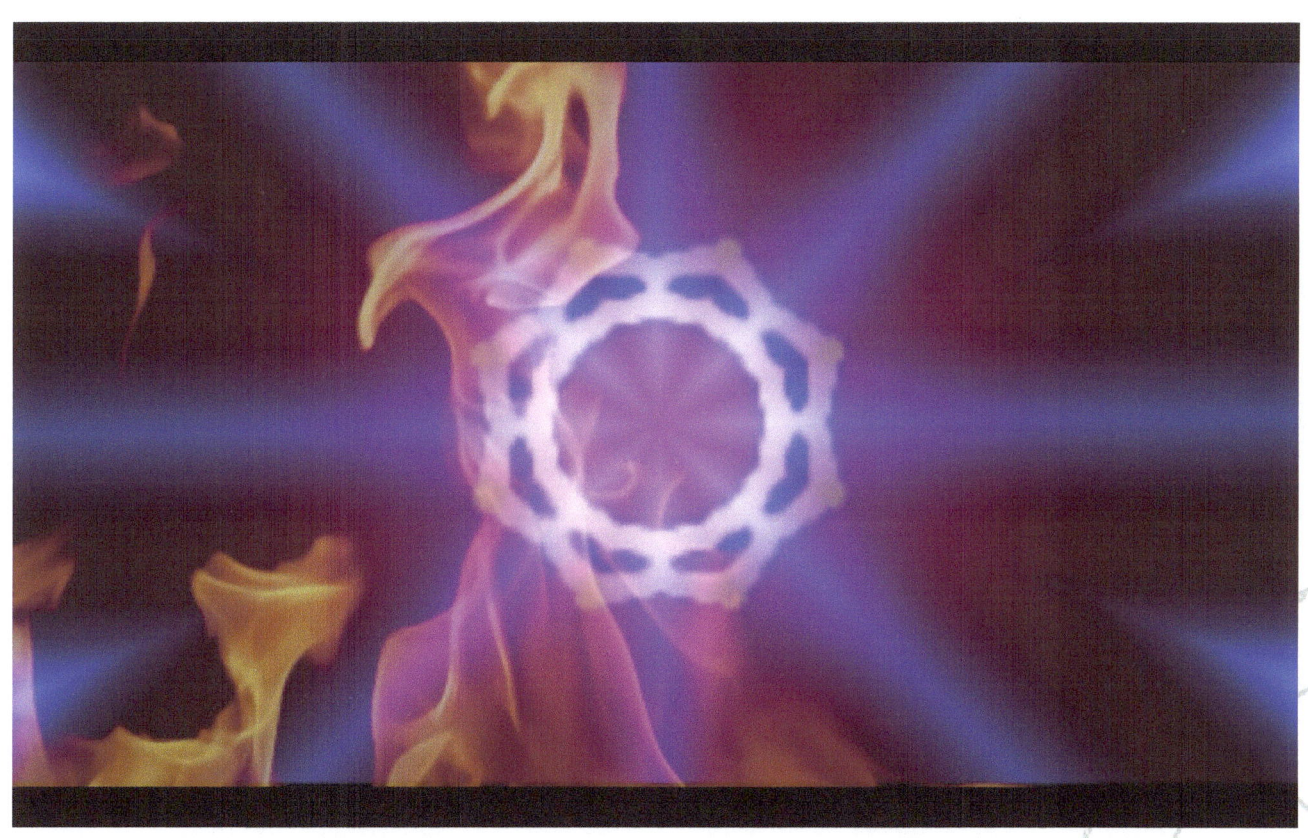

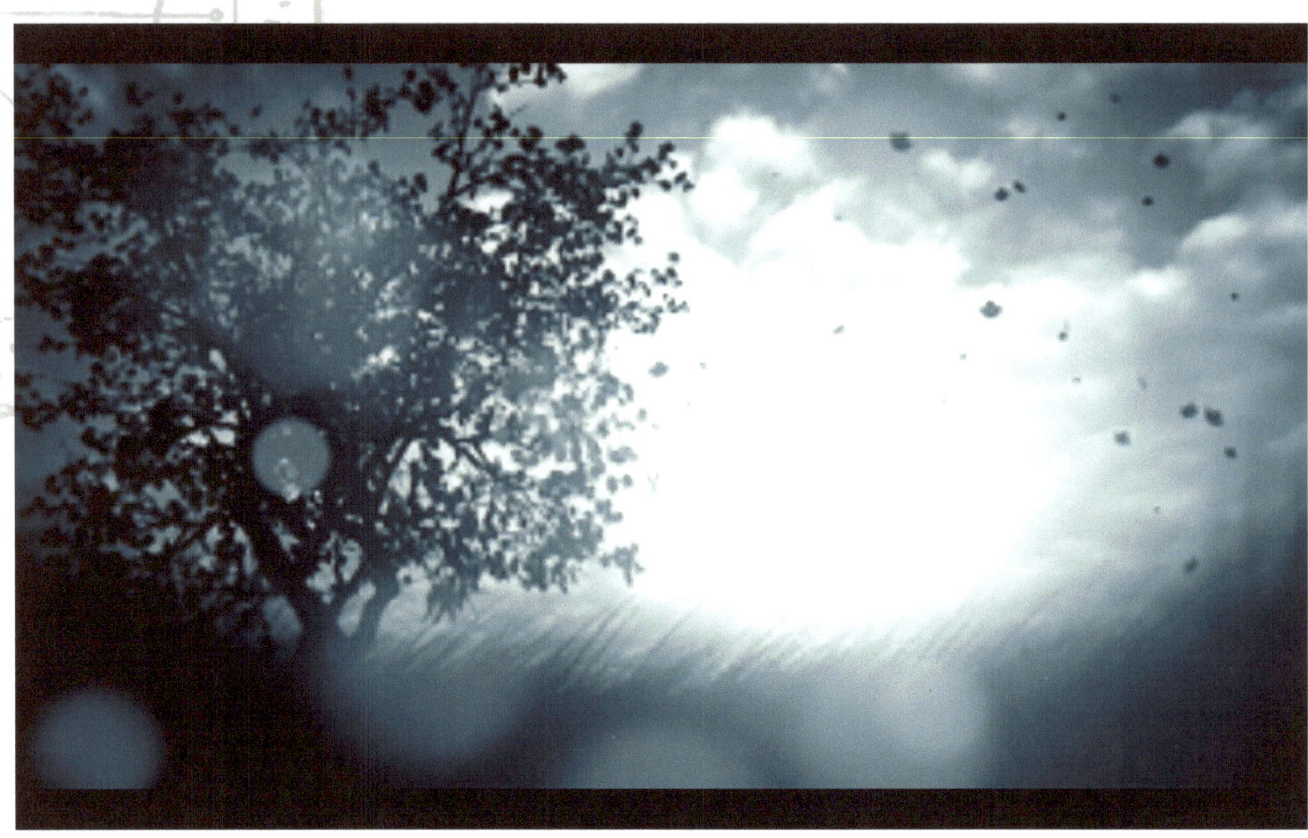

Coming Home short film 6.10 minutes

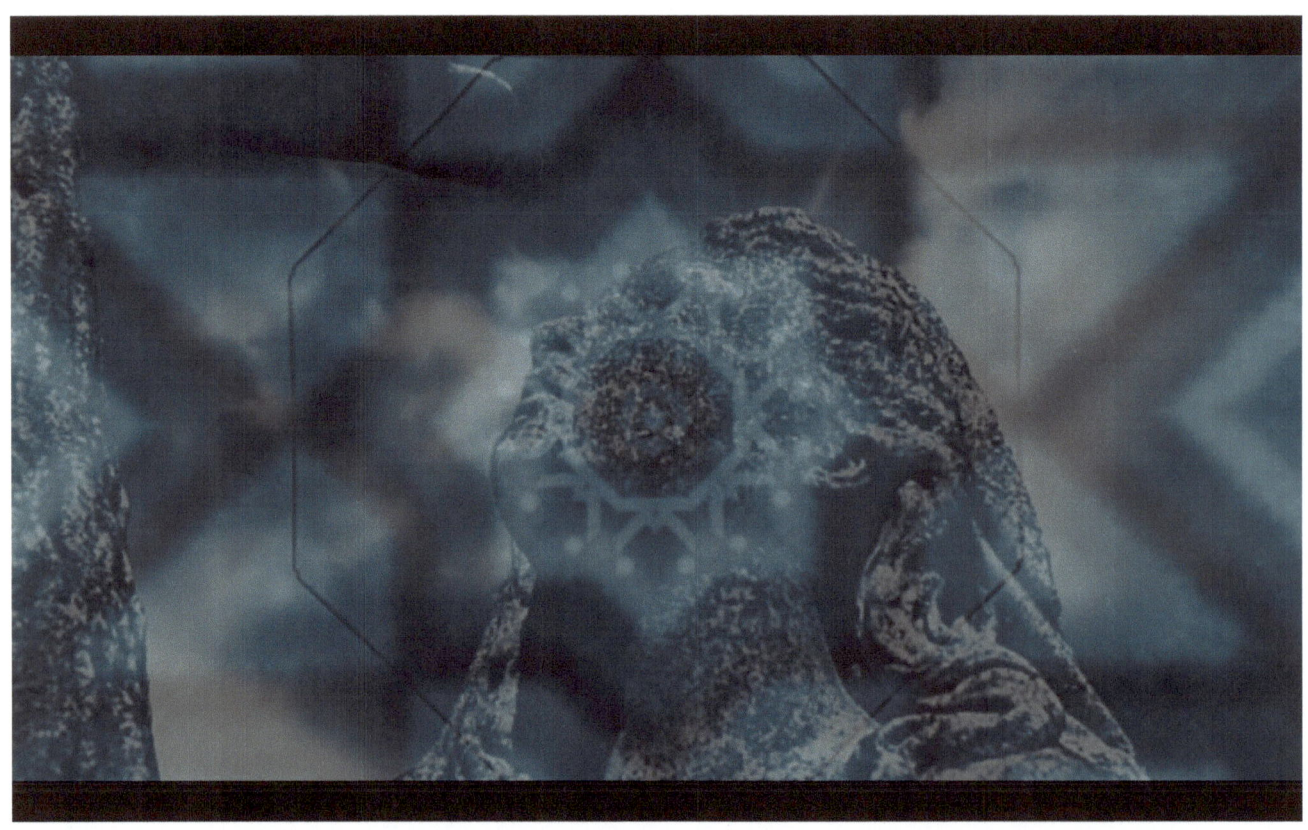

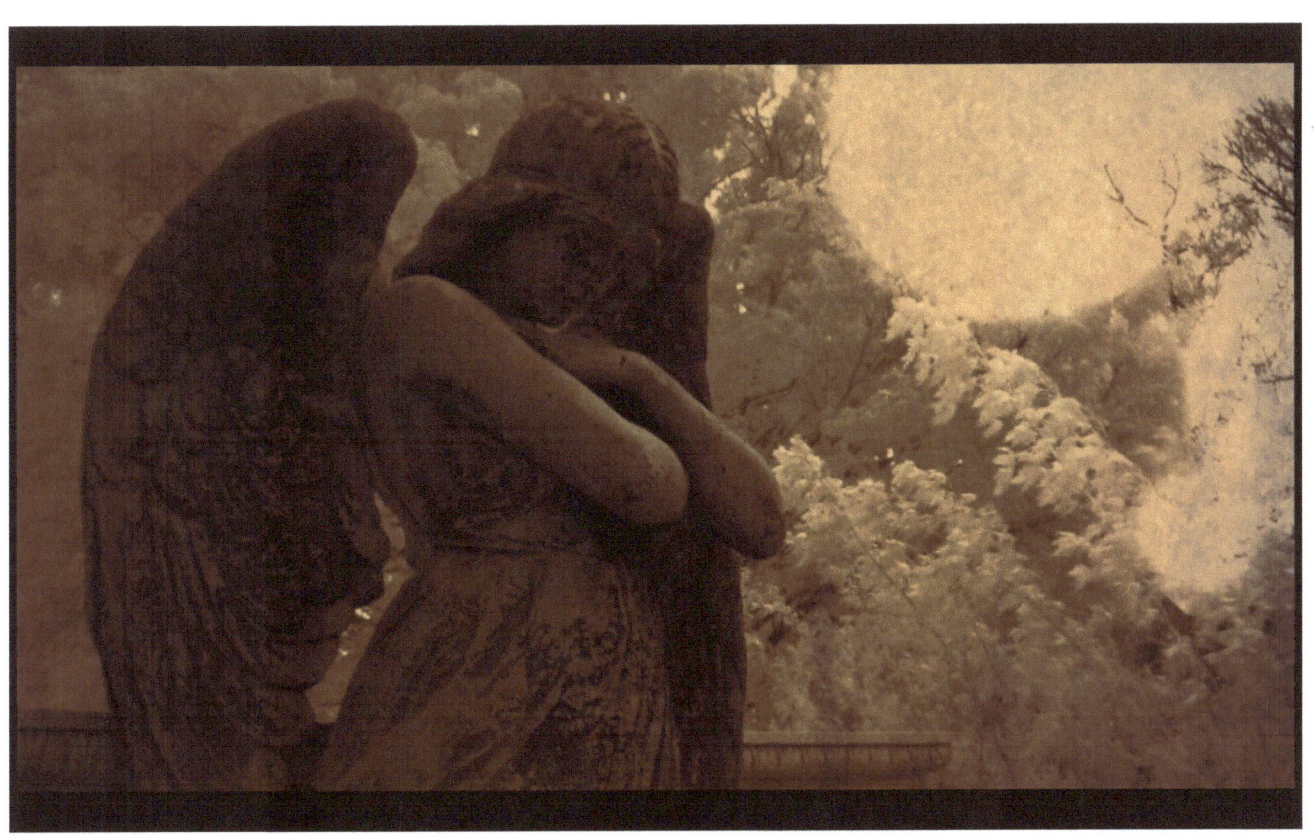

Walk with Me   short film   14.16 minutes

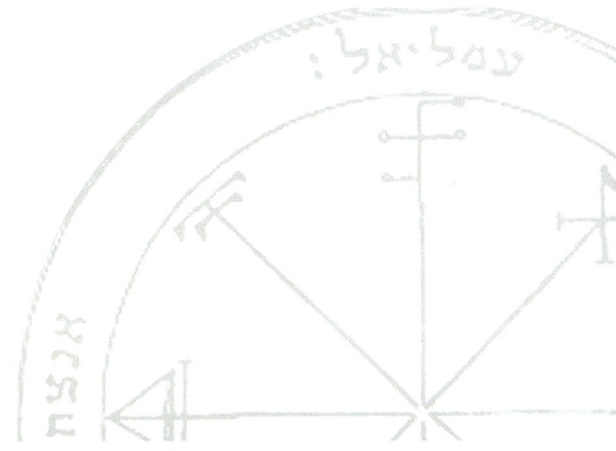

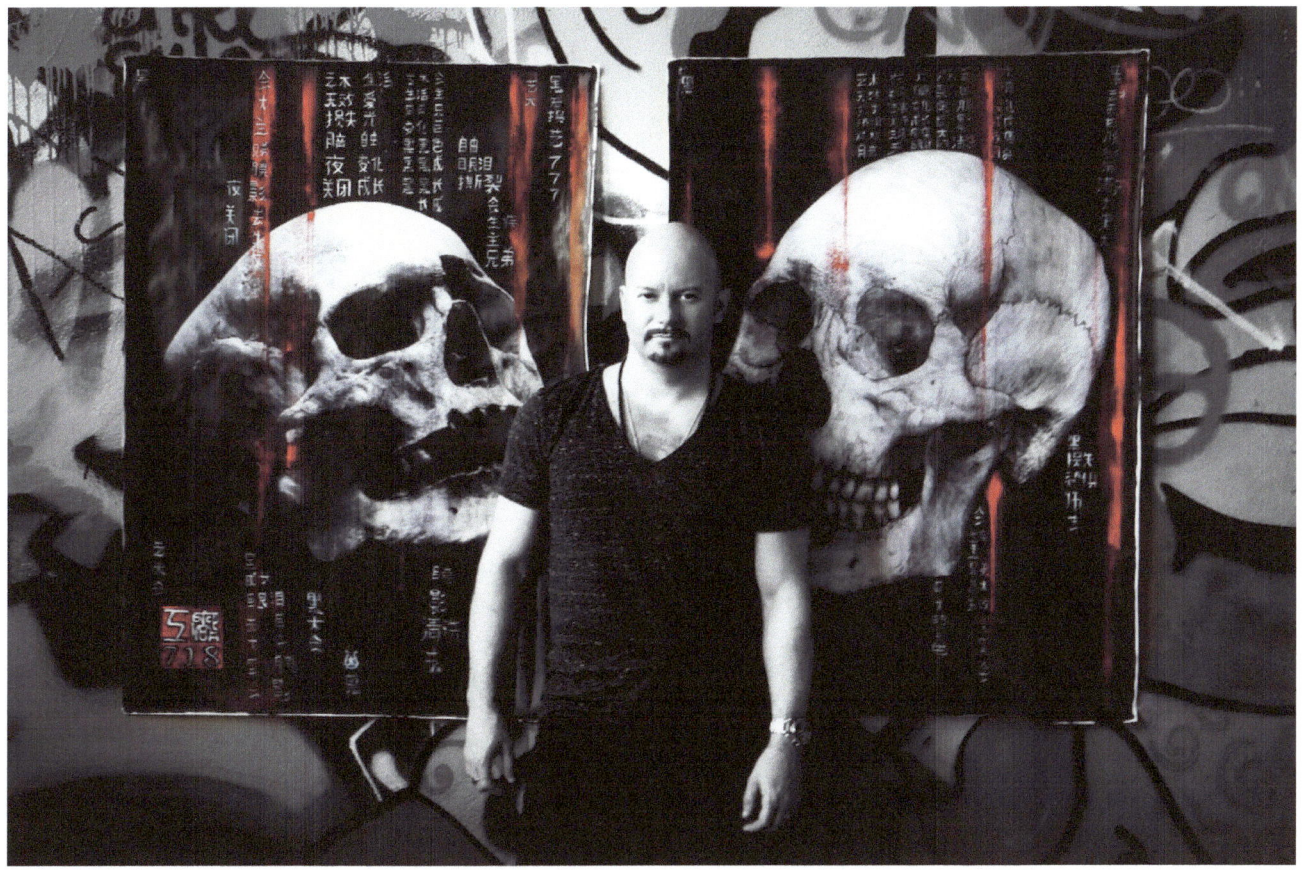

Artist Biography: Robert Buratti

Robert Buratti grew up with a strong interest in visual art from an early age and a fascination for the Renaissance masters. After graduating high school, he was awarded a Bachelor of Arts from Macquarie University with majors in english literature, cultural and critical theory and psychology. While studying he began his career working for a number of commercial art galleries in Sydney, before continuing to a Master of Arts Administration at the prestigious College of Fine Arts/ UNSW.

His work is chiefly concerned with the role of the spiritual within contemporary art, and the talismanic and tranformational power of the image. Influenced by the approach and experimentation of artists such as James Gleeson, Andre Breton, Aleister Crowley, Paul Gauguin and Pablo Picasso, his work seeks a balance between the seen and unseen, the technical and the intuitive. In 2007, he relocated to Western Australia, establishing his own fine art gallery in 2011. His work as a curator extends to both the commercial and public sector with such landmark exhibitions as The Nightmare Paintings, which brought the original paintings of Aleister Crowley to Australia for the first time, and the highly attended touring exhibition, Windows to the Sacred, at The National Trust of Australia/ S.H Ervin Gallery, both of which have become key events in the resurgence of interest in the genre of esoteric and outsider art in this country. Robert Buratti now lives in Perth, Western Australia where he balances his personal art practice with artist management and curation.

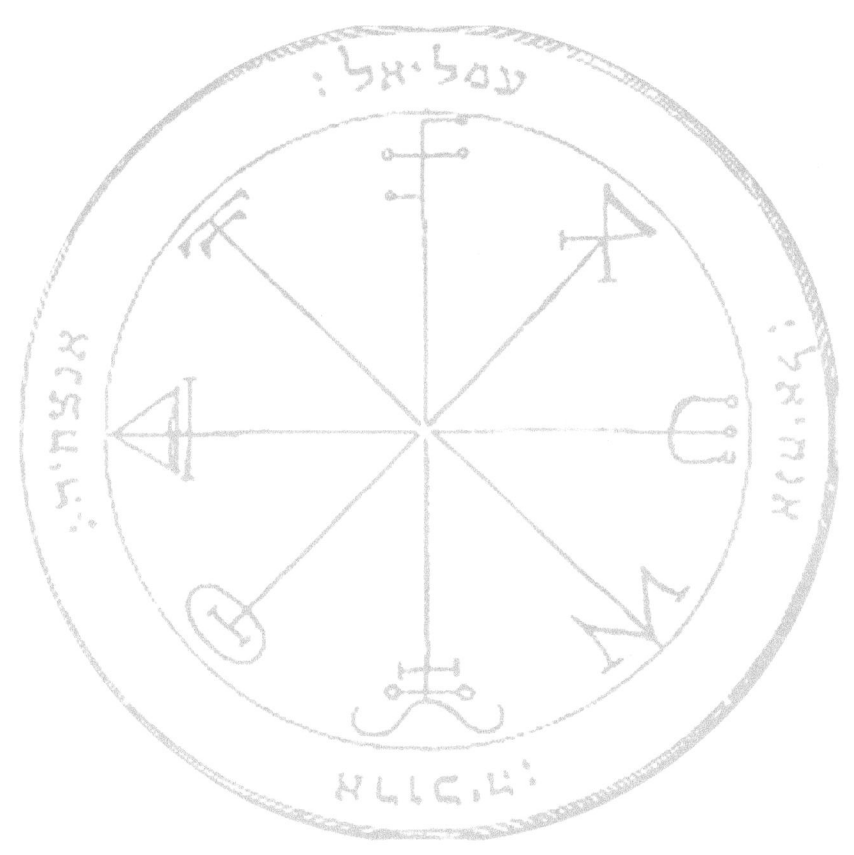